OPPOSING
VIEWPOINTS®
SERIES

Online Filter Bubbles

Other Books of Related Interest

Opposing Viewpoints Series

The Fifth Estate: Extreme Viewpoints from Alternative Media
Internet Censorship
Netiquette and Online Ethics
Net Neutrality

At Issue Series

Media Bias and the Role of the Press
Politicians on Social Media
Populism in the Digital Age
User-Generated Content

Current Controversies Series

Are There Two Americas?
Microagressions, Safe Spaces, and Trigger Warnings
Political Extremism in the United States
Politics and Media

> "Congress shall make no law … abridging the freedom of speech, or of the press."

First Amendment to the US Constitution

The basic foundation of our democracy is the First Amendment guarantee of freedom of expression. The Opposing Viewpoints series is dedicated to the concept of this basic freedom and the idea that it is more important to practice it than to enshrine it.

OPPOSING
VIEWPOINTS®
SERIES

Online Filter Bubbles

Paula Johanson, Book Editor

GREENHAVEN
PUBLISHING

Published in 2018 by Greenhaven Publishing, LLC
353 3rd Avenue, Suite 255, New York, NY 10010

Articles in Greenhaven Publishing anthologies are often edited for length to meet page
requirements. In addition, original titles of these works are changed to present clearly
the main thesis and to indicate explicitly the author's opinion. Every effort is made to
ensure that Greenhaven Publishing accurately reflects the original intent of the authors.
Every effort has been made to trace the owners of the copyrighted material.

Cover image: GaudiLab/Shutterstock.com

Library of Congress Cataloging-in-Publication Data

Names: Johanson, Paula, editor.
Title: Online filter bubbles / Paula Johanson, book editor.
Description: New York : Greenhaven Publishing, 2018. | Series: Opposing
 viewpoints | Includes bibliographical references and index. | Audience:
 Grades 9-12.
Identifiers: LCCN 2017038062| ISBN 9781534501751 (library bound) | ISBN
 9781534501812 (pbk.)
Subjects: LCSH: Information filtering systems--Juvenile literature. | Web
 browsing--Psychological aspects--Juvenile literature. | Internet
 searching--Psychological aspects--Juvenile literature. | Content analysis
 (Communication)--Juvenile literature.
Classification: LCC Z667.6 .O55 2018 | DDC 025.04--dc23
LC record available at https://lccn.loc.gov/2017038062

Manufactured in the United States of America

Website: http://greenhavenpublishing.com

Contents

The Importance of Opposing Viewpoints

Perhaps every generation experiences a period in time in which the populace seems especially polarized, starkly divided on the important issues of the day and gravitating toward the far ends of the political spectrum and away from a consensus-facilitating middle ground. The world that today's students are growing up in and that they will soon enter into as active and engaged citizens is deeply fragmented in just this way. Issues relating to terrorism, immigration, women's rights, minority rights, race relations, health care, taxation, wealth and poverty, the environment, policing, military intervention, the proper role of government—in some ways, perennial issues that are freshly and uniquely urgent and vital with each new generation—are currently roiling the world.

If we are to foster a knowledgeable, responsible, active, and engaged citizenry among today's youth, we must provide them with the intellectual, interpretive, and critical-thinking tools and experience necessary to make sense of the world around them and of the all-important debates and arguments that inform it. After all, the outcome of these debates will in large measure determine the future course, prospects, and outcomes of the world and its peoples, particularly its youth. If they are to become successful members of society and productive and informed citizens, students need to learn how to evaluate the strengths and weaknesses of someone else's arguments, how to sift fact from opinion and fallacy, and how to test the relative merits and validity of their own opinions against the known facts and the best possible available information. The landmark series Opposing Viewpoints has been providing students with just such critical-thinking skills and exposure to the debates surrounding society's most urgent contemporary issues for many years, and it continues to serve this essential role with undiminished commitment, care, and rigor.

The key to the series's success in achieving its goal of sharpening students' critical-thinking and analytic skills resides in its title—

Opposing Viewpoints. In every intriguing, compelling, and engaging volume of this series, readers are presented with the widest possible spectrum of distinct viewpoints, expert opinions, and informed argumentation and commentary, supplied by some of today's leading academics, thinkers, analysts, politicians, policy makers, economists, activists, change agents, and advocates. Every opinion and argument anthologized here is presented objectively and accorded respect. There is no editorializing in any introductory text or in the arrangement and order of the pieces. No piece is included as a "straw man," an easy ideological target for cheap point-scoring. As wide and inclusive a range of viewpoints as possible is offered, with no privileging of one particular political ideology or cultural perspective over another. It is left to each individual reader to evaluate the relative merits of each argument— as he or she sees it, and with the use of ever-growing critical-thinking skills—and grapple with his or her own assumptions, beliefs, and perspectives to determine how convincing or successful any given argument is and how the reader's own stance on the issue may be modified or altered in response to it.

This process is facilitated and supported by volume, chapter, and selection introductions that provide readers with the essential context they need to begin engaging with the spotlighted issues, with the debates surrounding them, and with their own perhaps shifting or nascent opinions on them. In addition, guided reading and discussion questions encourage readers to determine the authors' point of view and purpose, interrogate and analyze the various arguments and their rhetoric and structure, evaluate the arguments' strengths and weaknesses, test their claims against available facts and evidence, judge the validity of the reasoning, and bring into clearer, sharper focus the reader's own beliefs and conclusions and how they may differ from or align with those in the collection or those of their classmates.

Research has shown that reading comprehension skills improve dramatically when students are provided with compelling, intriguing, and relevant "discussable" texts. The subject matter of these collections could not be more compelling, intriguing, or urgently relevant to today's students and the world they are poised to inherit. The anthologized articles and the reading and discussion questions that are included with them also provide the basis for stimulating, lively, and passionate classroom debates. Students who are compelled to anticipate objections to their own argument and identify the flaws in those of an opponent read more carefully, think more critically, and steep themselves in relevant context, facts, and information more thoroughly. In short, using discussable text of the kind provided by every single volume in the Opposing Viewpoints series encourages close reading, facilitates reading comprehension, fosters research, strengthens critical thinking, and greatly enlivens and energizes classroom discussion and participation. The entire learning process is deepened, extended, and strengthened.

For all of these reasons, Opposing Viewpoints continues to be exactly the right resource at exactly the right time—when we most need to provide readers with the critical-thinking tools and skills that will not only serve them well in school but also in their careers and their daily lives as decision-making family members, community members, and citizens. This series encourages respectful engagement with and analysis of opposing viewpoints and fosters a resulting increase in the strength and rigor of one's own opinions and stances. As such, it helps make readers "future ready," and that readiness will pay rich dividends for the readers themselves, for the citizenry, for our society, and for the world at large.

Introduction

> "The global village that was once
> the internet has been replaced by
> digital islands of isolation that are
> drifting further apart each day. From
> your Facebook feed to your Google
> Search, as your experience online
> grows increasingly personalized, the
> internet's islands keep getting more
> segregated and sound proofed."
>
> —Mostafa M. El-Bermawy,
> "Your Filter Bubble Is
> Destroying Democracy,"
> Wired, November 18, 2016

The internet is a great equalizer among communications media. As long as a person has access to a computer and a connection, they can get to the world of the internet. The newest smartphone or computer is not needed, and there are computers for public use at libraries and schools. There are free public lessons in using computers and surfing the internet.

Even the ability to read and write is not essential. A person who can barely sound out letters or recognize a few logos or Chinese characters can still listen to music recordings and find some pictures and sound on simple websites. There is a lot of content to be found, no matter what a person is seeking.

All of this information is overwhelming! The internet is so vast that we need its content to be curated for us. Some information is organized on websites by people who created them. Search engines are special websites with programs that help users find content, searching for certain words or images. These programs filter information. Instead of just showing a list of all twenty-seven thousand or more websites that mention "Hawaii golf courses" in random order, the list begins with ones close to a user's location or that the user has already read. Social media websites do this filtering too and show people posts and stories similar to ones they like.

Filtering information allows us to save time, get informed about what matters to us, and find what we are looking for without wading through a lot of inappropriate material. Firewalls and filters can be set up on home computers or public computers to protect vulnerable people or to prevent crime. Firewalls and filters on internet servers instituted by governments, schools, and public libraries remove freedom to access everything. In England, filters are set up to block pornography sites. In China, firewalls keep out some information from other countries—particularly articles about political activism. Internationally, filters are used to track and prosecute pedophiles and child pornography creators.

After using a search engine or social media for a while, the information offered can be very filtered or personalized. That's useful if you're a professional musician wanting to keep informed about performances and industry news, for example. It's limiting if you're voting for the local mayor and have never heard about anyone running against her. Filtering creates an online echo chamber, trapping us in spaces that are comfortable. These bubbles of information reinforce what a person has already learned and done.

There are researchers studying how misinformation spreads in social networks. Their mathematical model looks at hoaxes and lies like viruses. People can become infected with ideas just like germs and can spread misinformation like disease. The Internet allows for very fast spreading of ideas both true and false, especially within circles of friends. But people don't fall for a hoax only because they read it on Facebook. A much more important factor in whether people are fooled is if they know what to do when they are presented with a new idea.

Do people know what is likely to be true? People can learn to ask, "Who benefits from telling me this story?" It's actually easy to check if an idea is possible, or likely, or proved true. People have to remember to check facts and consider their sources. The threshold for fact-checking does not depend on how fast a hoax is spreading; it depends on how gullible a person is and whether they know how to consider probability.

Not everyone is equally susceptible to lies. When the man who operates Disinformedia and its many fake news websites spoke to Laura Sydell of National Public Radio, he told her that he and his writers made up many stories that went viral during the 2016 US presidential election campaign. He said these hoaxes work because they fit into existing right-wing conspiracy theories. He and his writers have tried to write fake news stories to trick liberals, but they haven't proven to be as easily fooled.

Some experts claim that online filter bubbles are creating a divided America. In a wide variety of viewpoints organized into chapters titled "How Personalized Is Our Online World?" "How Do Online Filter Bubbles Affect The Information We Consume?" "How Do Online Filter Bubbles Affect The Choices We Make?" and "Is There Hope Of Bursting Online Filter Bubbles?" readers will become informed enough to make their own conclusions about the Internet's potential—both good and bad.

CHAPTER 1

How Personalized Is Our Online World?

Chapter Preface

The viewpoints in this chapter discuss "the internet of me"—the personalization of the internet to the extent that online filter bubbles are created—and also online filters that are instituted ostensibly for our protection. The viewpoints represent different facets of this topic but overall serve as an introduction to the topic of online filter bubbles.

There are issues of privacy as related to the personal information collected by online filters. Social media is now getting more personalized, particularly with geotagging a user's location. Some users view these features as fun or useful for social reasons, while others consider them dangerous and overstepping boundaries for privacy reasons.

Is the "internet of me" so personalized that it isolates us too much? Do we miss out on common experiences and information because perhaps there are no more experiences common to everyone?

> *"Those with the most consistent ideological views on the left and right have information streams that are distinct from those of individuals with more mixed political views— and very distinct from each other."*

Media Habits Can Polarize Political Views

Amy Mitchell, Jeffrey Gottfried, Jocelyn Kiley, and Katerina Eva Matsa

In the following viewpoint, Amy Mitchell, Jeffrey Gottfried, Jocelyn Kiley, and Katerina Eva Matsa argue that conservative and liberal Americans live in completely different spaces when it comes to the news they digest. The authors describe how news media habits affect a person's political views and lead to polarization. However, it is perhaps surprising that their findings indicate that it is very difficult to not be exposed to at least some dissenting views. At the Pew Research Center, Mitchell is director of journalism research, Gottfried is a staff writer, Kiley is associate director in research, and Matsa is a senior researcher.

As you read, consider the following questions:

1. What did the Pew Research Study aim to shed light on?
2. What source did 47 percent of conservatives report relying on for news about government and politics?
3. Who tends to rely on a greater number of media sources, liberals or conservatives, according to the viewpoint?

When it comes to getting news about politics and government, liberals and conservatives inhabit different worlds. There is little overlap in the news sources they turn to and trust. And whether discussing politics online or with friends, they are more likely than others to interact with like-minded individuals, according to a new Pew Research Center study.

The project—part of a year-long effort to shed light on political polarization in America—looks at the ways people get information about government and politics in three different settings: the news media, social media and the way people talk about politics with friends and family. In all three areas, the study finds that those with the most consistent ideological views on the left and right have information streams that are distinct from those of individuals with more mixed political views—and very distinct from each other.

These cleavages can be overstated. The study also suggests that in America today, it is virtually impossible to live in an ideological bubble. Most Americans rely on an array of outlets —with varying audience profiles—for political news. And many consistent conservatives and liberals hear dissenting political views in their everyday lives.

Yet as our major report on political polarization found, those at both the left and right ends of the spectrum, who together comprise about 20% of the public overall, have a greater impact on the political process than do those with more mixed ideological views. They are the most likely to vote, donate to campaigns and participate directly in politics. The five ideological groups in this analysis (consistent liberals, mostly liberals, mixed, mostly conservatives and consistent conservatives) are based on responses to 10 questions about a range of political values. That those who express consistently conservative or consistently liberal opinions have different ways of informing themselves about politics and government is not surprising. But the depth of these divisions—and the differences between those who have strong ideological views and those who do not—are striking.

Overall, the study finds that consistent conservatives:

- Are tightly clustered around a single news source, far more than any other group in the survey, with 47% citing Fox News as their main source for news about government and politics.
- Express greater distrust than trust of 24 of the 36 news sources measured in the survey. At the same time, fully 88% of consistent conservatives trust Fox News.
- Are, when on Facebook, more likely than those in other ideological groups to hear political opinions that are in line with their own views.
- Are more likely to have friends who share their own political views. Two-thirds (66%) say most of their close friends share their views on government and politics.

By contrast, those with consistently liberal views:

- Are less unified in their media loyalty; they rely on a greater range of news outlets, including some—like NPR and the New York Times—that others use far less.
- Express more trust than distrust of 28 of the 36 news outlets in the survey. NPR, PBS and the BBC are the most trusted news sources for consistent liberals.
- Are more likely than those in other ideological groups to block or "defriend" someone on a social network—as well as to end a personal friendship—because of politics.
- Are more likely to follow issue-based groups, rather than political parties or candidates, in their Facebook feeds.

Those with down-the-line conservative and liberal views do share some common ground; they are much more likely than others to closely follow government and political news. This carries over to their discussions of politics and government. Nearly four-in-ten consistent conservatives (39%) and 30% of consistent liberals tend to drive political discussions—that is, they talk about politics often, say others tend to turn to them for information rather than the reverse, and describe themselves as leaders rather than listeners in these kinds of conversations. Among those with mixed ideological views, just 12% play a similar role.

It is important to note, though, that those at either end of the ideological spectrum are not isolated from dissenting views about politics. Nearly half (47%) of across-the-board conservatives— and 59% of across-the-board liberals—say they at least sometimes disagree with one of their closest political discussion partners.

For those closer to the middle of the ideological spectrum, learning about politics, or discussing it with friends and family, is a less of a focus. When they do follow politics, their main news sources include CNN, local TV and Fox News, along with Yahoo News and Google News, which aggregate stories from a wide assortment of outlets; these U.S. adults see more of a mix of views in social media and are less likely to be aware of their friends' political leanings.

This study, the latest in a series of reports on political polarization, is based on an online survey conducted March 19-April 29, 2014 with 2,901 members of the Pew Research Center's new American Trends Panel—a panel recruited from a telephone survey of 10,013 adults conducted earlier this year.

Among the key findings:

Media Sources: Nearly Half of Consistent Conservatives Cite Fox News

When it comes to choosing a media source for political news, conservatives orient strongly around Fox News. Nearly half of consistent conservatives (47%) name it as their main source for government and political news, as do almost a third (31%) of those with mostly conservative views. No other sources come close.

Surfing the Data Tsunami

Due to the Data Tsunami created by the vast amount of information in [the] projected future, personalization will be required to focus content and allow people to navigate their own networks. Recommendation engines that compile our habits with our preferences will tailor our shopping, leisure and social experiences. People will know what events are going on, what food is being served, where meetings are happening, and where they most likely want to be at the touch of a screen. While this technology will show them exactly what they want to see, it begs the question: will they care about the information they are *not receiving*?

For arts organizations, this could lead to new levels of advertising, event management and customer service, but it will also require new levels of tech savvy and strategic media planning. Data is powerful and no organization wants to be on the wrong side of a filter.

Personalized recommendations, advertising, and marketing have already been implemented on sites like Google, Groupon, and Facebook. An individual's habits and data input affect the advertisements presented to them and the ways in which services are provided. In the future, this technology will become even more sophisticated and less conspicuous. The digital wave of news and information will manifest itself in total customization and intuitively targeted marketing.

Data input and manipulation could become a new burden for many institutions. In a world of customized lives and filtered data experiences, the arts will need to create their own space, partner with other industries and stake a claim in the entertainment and cultural markets. Being able to track events by location, recommend performances from purchasing habits and cultivate new donors from restaurant choices are wonderful concepts that could arise from this technology, but they will need to be created and managed by the arts institutions themselves.

"True Personalization: Don't Get Filtered," by Joe Frandoni, Master of Arts Management Program, October 21, 2010.

Consistent liberals, on the other hand, volunteer a wider range of main sources for political news—no source is named by more than 15% of consistent liberals and 20% of those who are mostly liberal. Still, consistent liberals are more than twice as likely as web-using adults overall to name NPR (13% vs. 5%), MSNBC (12% vs. 4%) and the New York Times (10% vs. 3%) as their top source for political news.

Among the large group of respondents with mixed ideological views, CNN (20%) and local TV (16%) are top sources; Fox News (8%), Yahoo News (7%) and Google News (6%) round out their top five sources.

Trust and Distrust: Liberals Trust Many, Conservatives Trust Few

At least as important as *where* people turn for news is *whose* news they trust. And here, the ideological differences are especially stark.

Respondents were asked whether they had heard of each of the 36 outlets listed in the accompanying graphic. For those they had heard of, they were asked about their trust—or distrust—in each source.

Liberals, overall, trust a much larger mix of news outlets than others do. Of the 36 different outlets considered, 28 are more trusted than distrusted by consistent liberals. Just eight earn higher shares of distrust than trust. Still, among those eight, the levels of distrust can be high: fully 81% of consistent liberals distrust Fox News, and 75% distrust the Rush Limbaugh Show.

Among consistent conservatives, by contrast, there are 24 sources that draw more distrust than trust. The same is true for 15 sources among those with *mostly* conservative views. And, of the eight outlets more trusted than distrusted by consistent conservatives, all but one, on balance, are distrusted by consistent liberals.

Also at play here is the degree to which people are more familiar with certain news sources than others. Some outlets such as CNN,

ABC News and Fox News, are recognized by at least nine-in-ten respondents, meaning that more respondents offer a view of these outlets one way or the other. Outlets currently occupying more niche markets, such as Politico, the Economist or BuzzFeed, are known by only about a third of respondents. Thus, while they may elicit strong views in one direction, the share of respondents weighing in is relatively small.

This section of the report looks in detail at news audiences and trust and distrust of outlets across ideological groups.

Social Media: Conservatives More Likely to Have Like-Minded Friends

In the growing social media space, most users encounter a mix of political views. But consistent conservatives are twice as likely as the typical Facebook user to see political opinions on Facebook that are mostly in line with their own views (47% vs. 23%). Consistent liberals, on average, hear a somewhat wider range of views than consistent conservatives—about a third (32%) mainly see posts in line with their own opinions.

But that doesn't mean consistent liberals necessarily embrace contrasting views. Roughly four-in-ten consistent liberals on Facebook (44%) say they have blocked or defriended someone on social media because they disagreed with something that person posted about politics. This compares with 31% of consistent conservatives and just 26% of all Facebook users who have done the same.

Consistent liberals who pay attention to politics on Facebook are also more likely than others to "like" or follow issue-based groups: 60% do this, compared with 46% of consistent conservatives and just a third (33%) of those with mixed views. And both the left and the right are more likely than others to follow political parties or elected officials: 49% of consistent conservatives and 42% of consistent liberals do so, compared with 29% of Facebook users overall.

Talking Politics: Dissenting Views Penetrate, but Less Frequently for the Ideologically Consistent

In personal conversations about politics, those on the right and left are more likely to largely hear views in line with their own thinking.

While only a quarter (25%) of respondents with mixed ideological views say most of their close friends share their own political views, that is true of roughly half (52%) of consistent liberals and two-thirds (66%) of consistent conservatives. And, when those who talk about politics are asked to name up to three people they most often talk to about politics, half (50%) of consistent conservatives name only individuals they describe as also being conservative—outpacing the 31% of consistent liberals who name only liberals.

At the same time, consistent liberals are more likely to stop talking to someone because of politics. Roughly a quarter (24%) have done so, compared with 16% of consistent conservatives and around 10% of those with more mixed political views.

Still, a solid portion of even the most ideologically-aligned respondents encounter some political disagreement with their close discussion partners. Nearly half (47%) of consistent conservatives who talk about politics name one or more discussion partners with whom they disagree at least some of the time. This figure rises to more than half (59%) of consistent liberals and even larger shares of those with mostly liberal and ideologically-mixed political views (79% each).

Media Outlets by the Ideological Composition of Their Audience

Ideological differences in media source preferences result in distinct audience profiles for many media outlets. Many sources, such as the Wall Street Journal, USA TODAY, ABC News, CBS News and NBC News have audiences that are, on average, ideologically similar to the average web respondent.

Reflecting liberals' use of a greater number of media sources, there are more outlets whose readers, watchers and listeners fall to the left of the average web respondent than to the right. At the same time, a handful of outlets have audiences that are more conservative than the average respondent.

Fox News sits to the right of the midpoint, but is not nearly as far right as several other sources, such as the radio shows of Rush Limbaugh or Glenn Beck. A closer look at the audience breakdowns reveals why: While consistent conservatives get news from Fox News at very high rates, many of those with less conservative views also use Fox News. By contrast, the audiences for Limbaugh and Beck are overwhelmingly conservative.

By comparison, the average consumer of the Wall Street Journal sits very close to the typical survey respondent, but the range of Journal readers is far broader because it appeals to people on both the left and the right. As a result, while respondents overall cluster toward the center of the ideological spectrum, the Journal's audience is relatively evenly distributed across the continuum: 20% are consistent liberals, 21% mostly liberal, 24% mixed, 22% mostly conservative and 13% consistent conservative.

> *"Curation does ideologically filter
> what we see. However, this effect
> is modest relative to choices people
> make that filter information."*

Social Algorithms Act as Ideological Filters

David Lazer

In the following viewpoint, David Lazer addresses the power of algorithms on our social media and internet use. Lazer compares Facebook to nineteenth-century Parisian salons, where philosophical, artistic, and other public issues were discussed. However, the author questions whether Facebook's curation process allows greater access to such forums or whether it undermines their quality. Because of ever more powerful algorithms, Facebook may prevent access to conflicting viewpoints for users. Lazer works in the Northeastern University Department of Political Science and College of Computer and Information Science.

As you read, consider the following questions:

1. How would I benefit from a customized experience when using social media?
2. How benign are the motivations for corporate decisions about personalized curation of social media?
3. Can we compare data-sorting choices made by filters to the choices people make on the Internet?

"The Rise of the Social Algorithm," by David Lazer, AAAS, May 7, 2015. Reprinted by permission.

Humanity is in the early stages of the rise of social algorithms: programs that size us up, evaluate what we want, and provide a customized experience. This quiet but epic paradigm shift is fraught with social and policy implications. The evolution of Google exemplifies this shift. It began as a simple deterministic ranking system based on the linkage structure among Web sites—the model of algorithmic Fordism, where any color was fine as long as it was black.[1] The current Google is a very different product, personalizing results[2] on the basis of information about past searches and other contextual information, like location. On page 1130 of this issue, Bakshy et al.[3] explore whether such personalized curation on Facebook prevents users from accessing posts presenting conflicting political views.

The rise of the social algorithm is rather less transparent than the post–Model T choice in automobiles. Today's social algorithms are so complex that no single person can fully understand them. It is illustrative in this regard to consider that Bakshy et al. are Facebook researchers studying the impact of Facebook algorithms. You might imagine that they could just go into the next building and look directly at the code. However, looking at the algorithms will not yield much insight, because the interplay of social algorithms and behaviors yields patterns that are fundamentally emergent. These patterns cannot be gleaned from reading code.

Social algorithms are often quite helpful; when searching for pizza in Peoria, it helps not to get results about Famous Ray's in Manhattan. However, personalization might not be so benign in other contexts, raising questions about equity, justice, and democracy. Bakshy et al. focus on the last, asking whether the curation of news feeds by Facebook undermines the role that Facebook plays as a forum for public deliberation.

For the Facebook-uninitiated, much of the activity of Facebook is in the form of news that users post to their feed, which their friends have some access to and can like and comment on. When you open Facebook, you see a list of recent posts by friends; however, you typically will not see all posts, which are algorithmically sorted.

The rationale for such curation is that in its absence, users would be deluged by uninteresting content from their friends. Facebook tries to pick out the gems from the detritus, anticipating what you will like and click on. But what are we missing? And are these computational choices troubling?

There are many facets to these questions, but one important one is how this curation affects Facebook as a deliberative sphere regarding public issues. Habermas[4] wrote of the role of the Parisian salons in the 19th century in offering a public space for such deliberations. The salons enabled intense conversation, with leakage across conversations creating a broader, systemic discussion. Facebook has many of these same qualities, and the issue is whether the curation process accentuates or undermines the quality of deliberation.

The specific deliberative issue that Bakshy *et al.* examine is whether Facebook's curation of news feeds prevents the intersection of conflicting points of view. That is, does a "filter bubble" emerge from this algorithmic curation process, so that individuals only see posts that they agree with?[5] Such an algorithmic sorting has the potential to be unhealthy for our democracy, fostering polarization and undermining the construction of a vision of the common good.

Their answer, after parsing the Facebook pages of ~10 million U.S. individuals with self-declared ideologies, is that the curation does ideologically filter what we see. However, this effect is modest relative to choices people make that filter information, including who their friends are and what they choose to read given the curation. The deliberative sky is not yet falling, but the skies are not completely clear either.

This is an important finding and one that requires continued vigilance. A small effect today might become a large effect tomorrow, depending on changes in the algorithms and human behavior. Ironically, these findings suggest that if Facebook incorporated ideology into the features that the algorithms pay attention to, it would improve engagement with content by removing dissonant ideological content. It is also notable, for example, that Facebook announced April 21st—well after the analysis conducted in this paper—three major changes to the curation of newsfeeds.

These changes had benign objectives, such as ensuring that one sees updates from "the friends you care about".[6] It is plausible, however, that friends that Facebook infers you to care about also tend to be more ideologically aligned with you as well, accentuating the filtering effect. Furthermore, the impact of curation on other dimensions of deliberative quality on Facebook remains to be examined. Open questions include whether the curation privileges some voices over others, and whether certain types of subjects are highlighted by the curation in a way that systematically undermines discussions of the issues of the day (pets over politics).

The impacts of social algorithms are a subject with rich scientific possibilities, not least because of the enormous data streams captured by these socio-technical systems.[7] It is not possible to determine definitively whether Facebook encourages or hinders political discussion across partisan divides relative to a pre-Facebook world, because we do not have nearly the same quality or quantity of data for the pre-Facebook world. The existence of Facebook, Twitter, etc., should be a boon to the study of political deliberation, because it is now possible to study these systems at a societal scale.

Important normative implications will follow from a clearer understanding of these systems. For example, a recent paper on price discrimination and steering that I coauthored[8] revealed that people sometimes get different prices and different products prioritized on e-commerce sites. This work has spurred substantial public discourse, as well as discussions with European Union regulators. Research such as that of Bakshy *et al.* has similar potential to inform a vigorous debate about the role that social media play in our society.

It is laudable that Facebook supported this research[3] and has invested in the public good of general scientific knowledge. Indeed, the information age hegemons should proactively support research on the ethical implications of the systems that they build.

Facebook deserves great credit for building a talented research group and for conducting this research in a public way. But there is a broader need for scientists to study these systems in a manner that is independent of the Facebooks of the world. There will be a need at times to speak truth to power, for knowledgeable individuals with appropriate data and analytic skills to act as social critics of this new social order.[9]

And although these systems are permeable and offer some entry points for study, this permeability is revocable and arguably decreasing. Facebook, for example, allows some access to user data via applications within the Facebook ecosystem. The relatively broad access creates the risk of third parties siphoning off large amounts of data from users, but has also allowed researchers to collect data to study Facebook.

The amount of data that can be collected via this route was sharply reduced on 30 April 2015[10] , with benefits to privacy, but undercutting independent research. This creates the risk that the only people who can study Facebook are researchers at Facebook— an unhealthy weighting of the dice of scientific exploration.

The fact that human lives are regulated by code is hardly a new phenomenon. Organizations run on their own algorithms, called standard operating procedures. And anyone who has been told that "it's a rule" knows that social rules can be as automatic and thoughtless as any algorithm. Our friends generally are a lot like us[11] and news media have always had to choose to pay attention to some stories and not others, in part based on financial and cultural imperatives.[12, 13] Social and organizational codes have always resulted in filter bubbles. However, every system of rules and every filtering process has potentially quite different dynamics and normative implications. Therein lies the most important lesson of Bakshy *et al.*'s report: the need to create a new field around the social algorithm, which examines the interplay of social and computational code.

Notes

1. S. Brin, L. Page, *Comput.Netw.ISDNSyst.*30,107(1998).

2. A.Hannak*etal.*,in*Proceedingsofthe22ndInternational Conference on World Wide Web* (International World Wide Web Conferences Steering Committee, Geneva, Switzerland, 2013), pp. 527–538.

3. E.Bakshy*etal.*,*Science*348,1130(2015).

4. J. Habermas, *The Structural Transformation of the Public Sphere: An Inquiry into a Category of Bourgeois Society* (MIT Press, Harvard, MA, 1991).

5. E. Pariser, *The Filter Bubble: What the Internet Is Hiding from You* (Penguin, London, 2011).

6. http://newsroom.fb.com/news/2015/04/news-feed-fyi-balancing-content-from-friends-and-pages

7. D. Lazer*etal.*, *Science*323,721(2009).

8. A. Hannak, G. Soeller, D. Lazer, A. Mislove, C. Wilson, in *Proceedings of the 2014 Conference on Internet Measurement Conference* (Association for Computing Machinery, New York, 2014), pp. 305–318.

9. Z. Tufekci, *First Monday* 10.5210/fm.v19i7.4901 (2014).

10. Go to https://developers.facebook.com/docs/apps/upgrading and click on "What happens on April 30, 2015".

11. M. McPherson*etal.*,*Annu.Rev.Sociol.*27,415(2001).

12. P. J. Shoemaker, T. P. Vos, *Gatekeeping Theory* (Routledge, NewYork, 2009).
    13. J. W. Dimmick, *Media Competition and Coexistence: The Theory of the Niche* (Erlbaum Associates, Mahwah, NJ, 2003).

> *"Once people have found 'evidence'
> of their views, external and
> contradicting versions are
> simply ignored."*

Confirmation Bias Allows the Spread of Misinformation Online

Walter Quattrociocchi

In the following viewpoint, Walter Quattrociocchi argues that misinformation spreads like wildfire online because, unlike with traditional media, there are no filters when individuals publish their own stories. The distribution potential may be equal, but the journalistic standards and quality control are not the same. That is the danger of the digital age. It is much easier to share and spread false stories and conspiracy stories. Even worse are findings that attempting to debunk fake news only reinforces believers' willingness to believe the falsehood. The author notes that fighting misinformation is a very difficult proposition. Quattrociocchi is head of the laboratory of computational social science at IMT Lucca in Italy.

As you read, consider the following questions:

1. What is an echo chamber?
2. How have online "trolls" evolved, according to the author?
3. How does even mentioning a correction make an error stronger?

"How Does Misinformation Tpread Online?" by Walter Quattrociocchi, World Economic Forum, January 14, 2016. Reprinted by permission.

I n the run up to the 2013 Italian elections, a social media post exposing the corruption of parliament went viral. Italian politicians were quietly certain that, win or lose, they would be financially secure by taking money from the taxpayer. Parliament had quietly passed a special welfare bill specially designed to protect policy-makers by ensuring them an incredible unemployment package should they lose their seat in the upcoming election. The bill, proposed by Senator Cirenga, allocated an amazing €134 billion to political unemployment. The Italian Senate had voted 257 in favour and 165 in abstention.

The post caused considerable and understandable uproar. It was covered in several leading newspapers and cited by mainstream political organizations. But there was one problem: the entire story was fake. Not even a good fake at that. For those interested in Italian politics, there were a number of obvious problems with the story. First of all, there is no Senator Cirenga. The number of votes doesn't work either, because Italy doesn't even have that many senators. And the incredible sum would have accounted for roughly 10% of Italy's GDP.

So what happened? How did such an obvious fake fool so many people?

Walter Quattrociocchi, the head of the Laboratory of Computational Social Science at IMT Lucca in Italy, has been studying the phenomenon of misinformation online. His work helped to inform the World Economic Forum's latest Global Risks Report. We spoke with him to find out more.

Why Is This Happening?

Before the web, you got your information from magazines, television and the newspapers. Now anyone can create a blog, have a Tumblr page or post their opinions online. From there, you can spread that information rapidly through Twitter, Facebook and a whole smorgasbord of other social media platforms.

The problem is that while traditional media had editors, producers and other filters before information went public,

Britain Implements Filters for Certain Content

Just three months ago, we at EFF expressed our disappointment with Australia's two largest Internet service providers (ISPs), Telstra and Optus, for agreeing to implement a filtering scheme after a filtering bill from the Australian government failed to pass.

The blocked sites were to include "the appropriate subsection of the Australian Communications and Media Authority (ACMA) blacklist as well as child abuse URLs that are provided by reputable international organisations," according to News.com.au. Now, in conjunction with the Christian organization Mothers' Union, UK Prime Minister David Cameron has decided to take similar measures, enacting a plan with four of Britain's major ISPs—BT, TalkTalk, Virgin, and Sky—to block access to pornography, gambling, self-harm, and other blacklisted websites. The "good news" is that the filtering isn't mandatory: New customers will be required to select between a filtered and unfiltered connection, while existing customers will be offered the same choice via email. The bad news, on the other hand, is extensive.

First, **the plan lacks transparency**. The blocked categories are vague in nature, and the list's origins unknown. Not only do the categories contain legal content in some cases, but there is significant room for overblocking. For example, one filtering tool used by several Middle Eastern governments categorizes Tumblr.com as pornography, because several pornographic blogs are hosted on the platform.

Second, **customers of ISP TalkTalk who opt out are still monitored**, says University of Cambridge security research Richard Clayton, who in May noted a series of privacy concerns relating to TalkTalk's use of the HomeSafe system, the same system the ISP intends to use for filtering. According to Clayton, "the company scans all web addresses that its customers visit regardless of whether they have opted-in to the service."

Third, **opt-in services create privacy concerns**. Users who choose to opt out of the "bad" content filter are then on one list. The plan does not in include privacy protections for the people who choose to opt out. The list could potentially be made public, shaming users who would prefer their Internet with its pornography, gambling, and self-harm websites intact...

> Time and time again, filtering based on blacklists has proven to be overbroad, blocking access to some offensive websites at the cost of many legitimate ones. Parents have plenty of Internet filtering options which they can implement by installing software on their computers at home.
>
> **"UK Enacts Filtering for Porn, Gambling, and Other Content," by Eva Galperin and Jillian C. York. Electronic Frontier Foundation, October 13, 2011.**

individual publishing has no filter. You simply say what you want and put it out there.

The result is that everyone can produce or find information consistent with their own belief system. An environment full of unchecked information maximizes the tendency to select content by confirmation bias.

Recent studies that focus on misinformation online pointed out that the selective exposure to specific content leads to "echo chambers" in which users tend to shape and reinforce their beliefs.

What Is an Echo Chamber?

An echo chamber is an isolated space on the web, where the ideas being exchanged essentially just confirm one another. It can be a space of likeminded people sharing similar political views, or a page about a specific conspiracy theory. Once inside one of these spaces, users are sharing information that is all very similar, basically "echoing" each other.

We have studied the dynamics inside a single echo chamber. What we found is that the most discussed content refers to four specific topics: environment, diet, health and geopolitics.

Content belonging to the different topics are consumed in a very similar way by users. Likes and shares remain more or less the same across topics.

If we focus on the comments section however, we notice a remarkable difference within topics. Users polarized on geopolitics are the most persistent in commenting, whereas those focused on diet are less persistent.

We also found that users "jump" from one topic to another. Once they begin to "like" something, they do this more and more, like a snowball effect. Once engaged in a conspiracy corpus, a user tends to join the overall conversation, and begins to "jump" from one topic to another. The probability increases with user engagement (number of likes on a single specific topic). Each new like on the same conspiracy topic increases the probability to pass to a new one by 12%.

What Kind of Rumours Are Spreading?

Pages about global conspiracies, chem-trails, UFOs, reptilians. One of the more publicized conspiracies is the link between vaccines and autism.

These alternative narratives, often in contrast to the mainstream one, proliferate on Facebook. The peculiarity of conspiracy theories is that they tend to reduce the complexity of reality. Conspiracy theories create (or reflect) a climate of disengagement from mainstream society and from officially recommended practices - e.g. vaccinations, diet, etc.

Among the most fascinating social dynamics observed is trolling. Before, trolls were mainly people who just wanted to stir up a crowd, but the practice has evolved. Trolls today act to mock the "believe anything" culture of these echo-chambers. They basically attack contradictions through parody.

Trolls' activities range from controversial and satirical content to the fabrication of purely fictitious statements, heavily unrealistic and sarcastic. For instance, conspiracist trolls aggregate in groups and build Facebook pages as a caricature of conspiracy news. A recent example was a fake publication of "findings" that showed chemtrails had traces of viagra in them.

What makes their activity so interesting is that, quite often, these jokes go viral and end up used as evidence in online debates from political activists.

How Have You Been Studying This Phenomenon?

On Facebook, likes, shares, and comments allow us to understand social dynamics from a totally new perspective. Using this data, we can study the driving forces behind the diffusion and consumption of information and rumours.

In our study of 2.3 million individuals, we looked at how Facebook users consumed different information at the edge of political discussion and news during the 2013 Italian elections. Pages were categorized, according to the kind of content reported on.

1. Mainstream media
2. Online political activism
3. Alternative information sources (topics that are neglected by science and mainstream media)

We followed 50 public pages and their users' interactions (like, comments and shares) for six months.

Each action has a particular meaning. A like gives positive feedback; a share expresses the will to increase the visibility; and comments expand the debate.

What we found was that neither a post's topic nor its quality of information had any effect on the outcome. Posts containing unsubstantiated claims, or about political activism, as well as regular news, all had very similar engagement patterns.

So People Are Reacting to Posts Based on Their Beliefs, Regardless of Where Those Posts Originated From?

Exactly. It's not that people are reacting the same way to all content, but that everyone is agreeing within their specific community.

People are looking for information which will confirm their existing beliefs. If today an article comes out from the WHO supporting your claims, you like it and share it. If tomorrow a new one comes out contradicting your claims, you criticise it, question it.

The results show that we are back to "echo chambers," there is selective exposure followed by confirmation bias.

To verify this, we performed another study, this time with a sample of 1.2 million users. We wanted to see how information related to very distinct narratives—i.e. mainstream scientific and conspiracy news—are consumed and shaped by communities on Facebook.

What we found is that polarized communities emerge around distinct types of content and consumers of conspiracy news tend to be extremely focused on specific content.

Users who like posts do so on the pages of one specific category 95% of the time. We also looked at commenting, and found that polarized users of conspiracy news are more focused on posts from their community. They are more prone to like and share posts from conspiracy pages.

On the other hand, people who consume scientific news share and like less, but comment more on conspiracy pages.

Our findings indicate that there is a relationship between beliefs and the need for cognitive closure. This is the driving factors for digital wildfires.

Does That Mean We Know What Will Go Viral Next?

Viral phenomena are generally difficult to predict. This insight does allow us to at least understand the users that are more prone to interact with false claims.

We wanted to understand if such a polarization in the consumption of content affects the structure of the user's friendship networks. In another study, Viral Misinformation: The role of homophily and polarization we found that a user's engagement in a specific narrative goes hand in hand with the number of friends having a similar profile.

That provides an important insight about the diffusion of unverified rumours. It means that through polarization, we can detect where misleading rumours are more likely to spread.

But Couldn't We Combat That by Spreading Better Information?

No. In fact, there is evidence that this only makes things worse.

In another study, we found that people interested in a conspiracy theory are likely to become more involved in the conversation when exposed to "debunking." In other words, the more the exposure to contrasting information a person is given, the more it reinforces their consumption pattern. Debunking within an echo chamber can backfire, and reinforce people's bias.

In fact, distrust in institutions is so high and confirmation bias so strong, that the Washington Post has recently discontinued their weekly debunking column.

What Can Be Done to Fight Misinformation?

Misinformation online is very difficult to correct. Confirmation bias is extremely powerful. Once people have found "evidence" of their views, external and contradicting versions are simply ignored.

One proposal to counteract this trend is algorithmic-driven solutions. For example, Google is developing a trustworthiness score to rank the results of queries. Similarly, Facebook has proposed a community-driven approach where users can flag false content to correct the newsfeed algorithm.

This issue is controversial, however, because it raises fears that the free circulation of content may be threatened and the proposed algorithms might not be accurate or effective. Often users denounce attempts to debunk false information, such as the link between vaccination and autism, as acts of misinformation.

> *"Minorities and those who are disadvantaged due to structural inequalities need special exposure to be able to reach out with their voice to larger publics."*

Filter Bubbles Are a Threat to Democracies

Engin Bozdag and Jeroen van den Hoeven

In the following excerpted viewpoint, Engin Bozdag and Jeroen van den Hoeven argue that online filter bubbles are a serious threat to democracies. The authors discuss the digital tools being developed to combat online filter bubbles. However, they contend, there are varying definitions of democracies, and the tools used to combat the algorithms that threaten them may not be designed to protect all democracies. Diversity in design of tools is needed to protect the diverse conceptions of democracy. Bozdag and van den Hoeven work in the faculty of values, technology, and innovation at Delft University of Technology in the Netherlands.

As you read, consider the following questions:

1. What is cyberbalkanization?
2. Why do liberals see filter bubbles as a problem, according to the viewpoint?
3. What is the view of politics for agonists?

"Breaking the Filter Bubble: Democracy and Design," by Engin Bozdag and Jeroen van den Hoven, Springer, December 18, 2015. http://www.firstamendmentcenter.org/t-shirt-rebellion-in-the-land-of-the-free/. Licensed Under BY CC 4.0.

Introduction

Cyberbalkanization refers to the idea of segregation of the Internet into small political groups with similar perspectives to a degree that they show a narrow-minded approach to those with contradictory views. For instance Sunstein (2007) argued that thanks to the Internet, people could join into groups that share their own views and values, and cut themselves off from any information that might challenge their beliefs. This, according to Sunstein, will have a negative effect on the democratic dialogue. Recently others have argued that personalization algorithms used by online services such as Facebook and Google display users similar perspectives and ideas and remove opposing viewpoints on behalf of the users without their consent (Pariser 2011). According to Pariser (2011), users might get different search results for the same keyword and those with the same friend lists can receive different updates. This is because information can be prioritized, filtered and hidden depending on a user's previous interaction with the system and other factors (Bozdag 2013; Diakopoulos 2014). This might lead to the situation in which the user receives biased information. In case of political information, it might lead to the situation that the user never sees contrasting viewpoints on a political or moral issue. Users will be placed in a "filter bubble" and they will not even know what they are missing (Pariser 2011). As a consequence, the epistemic quality of information and diversity of perspectives will suffer and the civic discourse will be eroded.

After Pariser's book has been published, the danger of filter bubbles received wide attention in the media, in academia and in industry. Empirical studies have been conducted to confirm or to debunk its existence. While algorithms and online platforms in general have been criticized because they cause filter bubbles, some designers have developed algorithms and tools to actually combat those bubbles. However, as we will show in this paper, the methods and goals of these tools differ fundamentally. Some try to give users full control and allow them to even increase their bubble. Some modify users' search results for viewpoint diversity without notifying the user. This is because the filter bubble has become a term that encompasses various criticisms. These criticisms differ because democracy is essentially a contested concept and different democracy models require different norms. As this paper will show, some will criticize the filter bubble due to its negative effect on user autonomy and choice, while others emphasize the diminishing quality of information and deliberation. In this paper we will show that while there are many different democracy theories, only the diversity related norms of a few of them are implemented in the tools that are designed to fight filter bubbles. We will also show that some norms (e.g., the inclusion of minorities in the public debate) are completely missing. We will argue that if we want to fully use the potential of the Internet to support democracy, all these diversity related norms should be discussed and designed, and not just the popular or most dominant ones.

In this paper, we first provide different models of democracy and discuss why he filter bubble pose a problem for these different models. Next, we provide a list of tools and algorithms that designers have developed in order to fight filter bubbles. We will do this by discussing the benchmarks these tools use and the democracy model the tools exemplify. We will show that not all relevant democracy models are represented in the overview of available diversity enhancing tools. Finally, we discuss our findings and provide some recommendations for future work.

Democracy and Filter Bubbles: Different Theories, Different Benchmarks

Democracy refers very roughly to a method of group decision making characterized by equality among the participants at an essential stage of the collective decision making (Christiano 2006). While some models of democracy emphasize the autonomy and individual preferences of those who take part in this collective decision making, others highlight the inclusion of free and equal citizens in the political community and the independence of a public sphere that operates as a middle layer between state and society (Habermas 1998). Some emphasize the need of an informed (online) debate and the epistemic quality of information before decisions are made (Hardin 2009). Others point out the need to increase the reach of minorities and other marginalized groups in the public debate (Young 2002).

While the filter bubble has been a concern for many, there are different answers to the question as to why filter bubbles are a problem for our democracy. The answer one gives to the question depends on one's understanding of the nature and value of democracy, on one's conception of democracy. Different democracy theories exist and they have different normative implications and informational requirements. A tool that implements one particular norm will be quite different in its form and goals than another tool which implements a different norm. Before we provide examples of different tools, we will provide a framework of some basic conceptions of democracy and the relevant norms for each model.

Liberal View of Democracy

The classical liberal view of democracy attempts to uphold the values of *freedom of choice, reason*, and *freedom from tyranny*, absolutism and religious intolerance (Dunn 1979; Held 2006) Liberalism started as a way to challenge the powers of "despotic monarchies" and tried to define a political sphere independent of church and state. Once liberalism achieved victory over these old "absolute powers," many liberal thinkers, began to express fear about the rising power of the "demos" (Madison 1787; Mill 1859; Held 2006). They were concerned by the new dangers to liberty posed by majority rule against minorities and the risk of the majority "tyrannizing over itself," leading to a need for people to "limit their power over themselves."

Bentham (1780) argues that, since those who govern will not act the same way as the governed, the government must always be accountable to an electorate called upon frequently and this electorate should be able to decide whether their objectives have been met. Next to voting, 'competition' between potential political representatives, "separation of powers," "freedom of the media, speech and public association" should be ensured to sustain "the interest of the community in general" (Bentham 1780). Individuals must be able to pursue their interests without the risk of arbitrary political interference, to participate freely in economic transactions, to exchange labor and goods on the market and to appropriate resources privately.

The liberal view of democracy is often criticized, because it construes democracy as an aggregation of individual preferences through a contest (in the form of voting), so that the preferences of the majority win the policy battle. However, this model has no way of distinguishing normatively legitimate outcomes from the preferences and the desires of the powerful, and makes no distinction between purely subjective preferences and legitimate and shared (quasi objective) judgments (Cohen 1997, 2009; Young 2002).

Filter bubbles are a problem according to the liberal view, because the non-transparent filters employed by online algorithms limit the *freedom of choice*. In addition, the liberal view states that citizens must be *aware* of different opinions and options, in order to make a *reasonable* decision. A filter imposed on users—unbeknownst to them—will violate their autonomy, as it will interfere with their ability to choose freely, and to be the judge of their own interests. Further, the principle of *separation of powers* and the *freedom of the media* can also be in danger, if the algorithms are designed in such a manner as to serve the interests of certain individuals or groups. Finally, filters might damage the "liberty of thought." Liberty of thought, discussion and action are the necessary conditions for the development of independence of mind and autonomous judgment. Liberty of thought creates reason and rationality, and in turn the cultivation of reason stimulates and sustains liberty. If one is "coerced" by the filters, reason will also diminish. While some thinkers such as Mill (1859) also emphasize the diversity of opinion, most liberal thinkers do not mention this as a requirement. Liberal citizens must be 'potentially' informed so that the elected act accountably, but deliberation according to the liberal view is not necessary. Loss of autonomy caused by filters seems to be the main issue, according to the liberal view, while diversity of opinions and perspectives is not a concern.

Deliberative Democracy

Elster (1997) characterizes deliberative democracy as "decision making by discussion among free and equal citizens." Deliberative democrats propose that citizens address societal problems and matters of public concern by reasoning together about how to best solve them. This can be made possible by deliberative procedures, which help to reach a moral consensus that satisfies both rationality (defense of liberal rights) and legitimacy (as represented by popular sovereignty) (Gutmann and Thompson 2004). Individuals participating in the democratic process can change their minds and preferences as a result of reflection. According to Cohen (2009), deliberative democracy can be seen (1) as a matter of forming a public opinion through open public discussion and translating that opinion into legitimate law; (2) as a way to ensure elections are themselves infused with information and reasoning; (3) as a way to bring reasoning by citizens directly to bear on addressing regulatory issues. In all cases the goal is to use the common reason of equal citizens who are affected by decisions, policies or laws, instead of having them enter into bargaining processes or represent them by means of the aggregation of their individual preferences. Democracy, no matter how fair, no matter how informed, no matter how participatory, does not qualify as deliberative unless reasoning is central to the process of collective decision-making.

There are different versions of deliberative democracy. Rawls' (1971, 1997) conception of deliberation is based on the idea of *public reason*, which is defined as "the basic moral and political values that are to determine a constitutional democratic government's relation to its citizens and their relation to one another." By means of public deliberation, people settle their disputes with respect and mutual recognition towards each other. Habermas (1998) provides similar conditions in his concept of the "ideal speech situation."The Rawlsian approach aims at "accommodation" of differences in a pluralistic society without criticizing people's fundamental views of life, their so- called "comprehensive doctrines" or "bringing them into deliberative discussion." Habermas' approach does the opposite, by also making moral or philosophical ideas and ideals part of the deliberative challenge. Both Rawls and Habermas advocate a "rational consensus" rather than "mere agreement" in political deliberation. For this purpose, Rawls uses the term "reasonable," and Habermas introduces the notion of "communicative rationality."

There are different versions of deliberative democracy. Rawls' (1971, 1997) conception of deliberation is based on the idea of public reason, which is defined as "the basic moral and political values that are to determine a constitutional democratic government's relation to its citizens and their relation to one another." By means of public deliberation, people settle their disputes with respect and mutual recognition towards each other. Habermas (1998) provides similar conditions in his concept of the "ideal speech situation."The Rawlsian approach aims at "accommodation" of differences in a pluralistic society without criticizing people's fundamental views of life, their so-called "comprehensive doctrines" or "bringing them into deliberative discussion." Habermas' approach does the opposite, by also making moral or philosophical ideas and ideals part of the deliberative challenge. Both Rawls and Habermas advocate a "rational consensus" rather than "mere agreement" in political deliberation. For this purpose, Rawls uses the term "reasonable," and Habermas introduces the notion of "communicative rationality."

Deliberative democrats argue that deliberation (1) enlarges the pools of *ideas* and *information* (Cohen 2009), (2) helps us discover *truths* (Manin 1997; Talisse 2005), (3) can lead us to a better grasp of *facts* (Hardin 2009), (4) can lead us to discover diverse *perspectives*, practical stances towards the social world that are informed by experiences that agents have (Bohman 2006),

(5) can help us discover the seriousness of our *disagreements* and discover that there is a disagreement after all (Cohen 1986), (6) can lead to a *consensus* on the "better or more "reasonable" solution (Landemore 2012), (7) promotes *justice*, as it requires full information and equal standing, (8) lead to better epistemic *justification* and *legitimacy* than simply voting (Hardin 2009). This is because political decisions based on deliberation are not simply a product of power and interest. It involves public reasons to justify decisions, policies or laws, (9) lead to *better arguments*, since citizens have to defend their proposals with reasons that are capable of being acknowledged as such by others (Cohen 2009), (10) allows citizens to *reflect* on their own arguments, that will lead to self-discovery and *refined arguments* (Cohen 1986), (11) promotes *respect*, as it requires people to consider the opinions of others, despite fundamental differences of outlook (Hardin 2009).

Critics of deliberative democracy argue that full fledged deliberation is difficult to attain because (1) there is inequality in deliberative capabilities of citizens, which gives advantages to the rhetorically gifted and those who possess cultural capital and argumentative confidence in leading the discussions (Ahlström 2012), (2) there is widespread incompetence and political ignorance among the masses (Ahlström 2012), (3) voters are not interested in the common good, but only in self-interests (Caplan 2008), (4) people are biased and may hold beliefs without investigation. Majority rule will amplify these mistakes and make democratic decisions worse (Caplan 2008), (5) while participation of citizens is possible in small nations, vast numbers of people will inevitably entail deterioration of participation (Held 2006). Past a certain threshold, deliberation turns into a chaotic mess (Landemore 2012), (6) most citizens cannot spend the time to master the issues well enough to take meaningful stands on major issues. The information processing cost and transaction cost is too high (den Hoven 2005), (7) deliberation among like-minded users can cause polarization. When people deliberate on a relatively homogenous argument pool, they consolidate fairly easily, which is bad for outsiders. Evidence from social psychology suggests that it is the viewpoints of the majority, not of the informed minorities, that can be expected to drive the relevant group judgments (Ahlström 2012). The informed minorities may refrain from disclosing what they know due to social pressure and be reluctant to dissent, thus not submitting the information to deliberation (Sunstein 2007), (8) forcing participants to deliberation with limiting their arguments due to commonly shared rational premises, public reason or common good will prevent dissenting voices to share their perspectives and identities on their own terms (Young 2002).

Filter bubbles are a problem for deliberative democrats, mainly because of the low quality of information and the diminishing of information diversity. If bubbles exist, the pool of available information and ideas will be less diverse and discovering new perspectives, ideas or facts will be more difficult. If we only get to see the things we already agree with on the Internet, discovering disagreement and the unknown will be quite difficult, considering the increasing popularity of the Internet and social media as a source of political information and news (Mitchell et al. 2014). Our arguments will not be refined, as they are not challenged by opposing viewpoints. We will not contest our own ideas and viewpoints and as a result, only receive confirming information. This will lead us not to be aware of disagreements. As a consequence, the quality of arguments and information and respect toward one other will suffer.

Republicanism and Contestatory Democracy

In contemporary political theory and philosophy, republicanism focuses on political liberty, understood as non-domination or independence from arbitrary power. The republican conception of political liberty defines freedom as a sort of structural independence—as the condition of not being subject to arbitrary or uncontrolled power. Pettit (1999) argues that people are free to the extent that no other group has "the capacity to interfere in their affairs on an arbitrary basis." To ensure that, according to Pettit (1999), there must be *an* "active, concerned citizenry who invigilate the exercise of government power, challenge its abuses and seek office where necessary." In this theory, freedom as non-domination supports a conception of democracy where contestability takes the place usually given to consent. The most important implication is not that the government does what the people want, but that people can always contest whatever decision the government has taken. While the republican tradition does not overlook the importance of democratic participation, the primary focus is clearly on avoiding the evils associated with interference and oppression.

Pettit (1999) argues that the media has a major role in forming the public opinion, ensuring non-domination and the possibility of effective contestation. However, Pettit argues, the media often fail badly in performing these roles. According to Pettit, at every site of decision-making (legislative, administrative and judicial), there must be procedures in place to identify and display the considerations relevant to the decision. The citizens should be able to contest these decisions if they find that the considerations did not actually determine the outcome. The decisions must be made under transparency, under threat of scrutiny, and under freedom of information. A group, even if they are a minority, should be able to voice contestation and must be able to speak out in a way that is liable to affect the proposed legislation. They must be able to contest in an effective manner, and they must be able to make themselves heard in decision-making quarters. To provide this, there must be reliable channels of publicity and information in place, so that the performance of the governing parties is systematically brought to attention.

If we apply these norms to the design of online platforms, we can argue that online information platforms (1) must make the right information available to the citizens and should allow them to track when something important or relevant happens. In this way, citizens can become aware of possible oppression and can become active when they feel there is a need to. This can for instance be achieved by human curation that aims at including important events that might affect the whole of society, in the information diet of everyone. It can also be achieved by means of personalization, so that, an event that is particularly important for a user can be highlighted for that user, (2) provide effective methods of contestation, so that citizens can make themselves heard with their contestations and affect the proposed legislation or policy. This means that people should not only be able to contest, but also that the contestation should reach a large public so that it can result in an effective and inclusive discussion.

Filter bubbles are a problem for advocates of contestatory democracy, because they interfere with realization of both conditions mentioned above. Bubbles both block the incoming and outgoing information channels. In order to raise critical questions, one must be aware of something that is a candidate for contestation. Someone cannot protest if they do not know that things relevant to them are happening. A filter bubble can block the reliable channels of publicity and information and may increase the risk that citizens are unaware of important news. Filter bubbles prevent awareness of both the items that people could disagree with and the information on the basis of which they could justify their reasons for disagreeing. Furthermore it may turn out to be much more difficult to communicate and share ideas with *potentially* like minded others outside your filter bubble. For not every post or comment on Facebook will reach your followers and a website with key information might never make it to the top of one's Google's search results.

Agonism/Inclusive Political Communication

While most deliberative democracy models aim for consensus concerning a "common interest," agonists see politics as a realm of conflict and competition and argue that disagreement is inevitable even in a well-structured deliberative democratic setting, and even if the ideal of consensus regulates meaningful dialogues (Mouffe 2009). According to these critics, different and irreconcilable views will coexist and an overlapping final consensus can never be achieved. Having consensus as the main goal and the refusal of a vibrant clash of democratic but opposing political positions will lead to "apathy and disaffection with political participation" (Mouffe 1999; Young 2002). According to Mouffe (2009), the aim of democratic politics according to advocates of this agonistic conception of democracy should not be seen as overcoming conflict and reaching consensus, because such a consensus would actually be a consensus of the hegemony.

The aim of "agonistic pluralism" then, is to construct the "them"(opposing viewpoint) in such a way that it is no longer perceived as an enemy to be destroyed, but as an "adversary." Thus, conflict must be in center stage in politics and it must only be contained by democratic limits.

An adversary is "somebody whose ideas we combat but whose right to defend those ideas we do not put into question" (Mouffe 2009). Agonistic pluralism requires providing channels through which collective passions will be given ways to express themselves over issues which, while allowing enough possibility for identification, will not construct the opponent as the enemy. The difference with "deliberative democracy" is that "agonistic pluralism" does not eliminate passions from the sphere of the public, in order to reach a consensus, but mobilizes those passions towards democratic designs. Democracy should then be designed so that conflict is accommodated and unequal power relations and hegemony in the society is revealed.

Mouffe (1999) argues that although the advocates of deliberative democracy claim to address pluralism and the complexity of the society, their reference to reason and rationality tends to exclude certain groups from the political arena; therefore, they are essentially not pluralistic.

Similarly, Young (2002) argues that if consensus becomes the ultimate goal, some difficult issues or issues that only concern a minority might be removed from discussion for the sake of agreement and preservation of the common good (Young 2002).

The idea of a generalized and impartial public interest that transcends all difference, diversity and division is problematic, because the participants in a political discussion most likely differ in social position or culture. Our democracies contain structural inequalities (e.g., wealth, social and economic power, access to knowledge, status). Some groups have greater material privilege than others, or there might be socially or economically weak minorities. Therefore in such settings "the common good" is likely to express the interests and perspectives of the dominant groups (Young 2002). The perspectives and demands of the less privileged may be asked to be put aside for the sake of a common good whose definition is biased against them.

Young (2002) argues that when there are structural conflicts of interest which generate deep conflicts of interest, processes of political communication are more about struggle than about agreement. However, according to Young, the field of struggle is not equal; some groups and sectors are often at a disadvantage. Fair, open, and inclusive democratic processes should then attend to such disadvantages and institutionalize compensatory measures for exclusion. Democratic institutions and practices must take measures explicitly to include the representation of social groups, relatively small minorities, or socially or economically disadvantaged ones. Disorderly, disruptive, annoying, or distracting means of communication are often necessary or effective elements in such efforts to engage others in debate over issues and outcomes. Christiano (2006) argues that due to cultural differences in society, deep cognitive biases make individuals fallible in understanding their own and other's interests and compare the importance of others' interest with their own. By default, people will fail to realize equal advancement of interests in society. Thus, special measures must be taken to make sure that equality is satisfied.

Filter bubbles are a problem for agonists and supporters of inclusive political communication, because they hide or remove channels through which opposing viewpoints can clash vibrantly. Minorities, and those who are disadvantaged due to structural inequalities need special exposure to be able to reach out with their voice to larger publics. However, filters that show us what we already agree with usually do not include such minority voices. If filters only show us what they consider "relevant" for us, then, the only way to reach a large public will be through advertisements or by gaming the filters. This will violate the inclusion norm of modern democracies, as only the wealthy who can afford such advertisements, or technologically advanced minds who can use algorithms to their own advantage will be able to express themselves.

References

Ahlström, K. (2012). Why deliberative democracy is (still) untenable. *Public Affairs Quarterly*, 26(3). http://philpapers.org/rec/AHLW DD-3.

Bentham, J. (1780). *An introduction to the principles of morals and legislation.* http://www. econlib.org/library/Bentham/bnthPML. html.

Bohman, J. (2006). Deliberative democracy and the epistemic benefits of diversity. *Episteme, 3*(03), 175–191. doi:10.3366/epi.2006.3. 3.175.

Bozdag, E. (2013). Bias in algorithmic filtering and personalization. *Ethics and Information Technology*, 15(3), 209–227.

Caplan, B. (2008). *The myth of the rational voter: Why democracies choose bad policies.* New edition. Princeton, NJ; Woodstock: Princeton University Press. http://www. amazon.com/The-Myth-Rational-Voter-Democracies/dp/0691138737.

Christiano, T. (2006). Democracy. Stanford Encyclopedia of Philosophy, July 27. http:// plato.stanford.edu/entries/democracy/. Cohen, J. (1986). An epistemic conception of democracy. *Ethics*, 97(1), 26–38. http://www.jstor.org/stable/2381404.

Cohen, J. (1997). Deliberation and democratic legitimacy. In J. Bohman & W. Rehg (Eds.), *Deliberative democracy: Essays on reason and politics.* Cambridge: MIT Press.

Cohen, J. (2009). Reflections on Deliberative Democracy. In T. Christiano & J. Christman (Eds.), *Contemporary debates in political philosophy.* West-Sussex: Blackwell.

Diakopoulos, N. (2014). *Algorithmic accountability reporting: On the investigation of black boxes.* Tow Center for Digital Journalism Brief, Columbia University. http://scholar. google.com/scholar?hl=en&btnG=Search&q=intitle:ALGORITHMIC?ACCOUNTA BILITY?REPORTING?:?ON?THE?INVESTIGATION?OF?BLACK?BOXES#0.

Dunn, J. (1979). *Western political theory in the face of the future* (Vol. 3). Cambridge: Cambridge University Press. http://books.google.nl/books /about/Western_Political_ Theory_in_the_Face_of.html?id=vw3tKOTVG0AC&pgis=1.

Elster, J. (1997). The market and the forum: Three varieties of political theory. In J. Bohman & W. Rehg (Eds.), *Deliberative democracy: Essays on reason and politics* (pp. 3–34). Cambridge: The MIT Press. doi:10.1177/019145370102700505.

Habermas, J. (1998). *Between facts and norms: Contributions to a discourse theory of law and democracy.* Cambridge: MIT Press. http://books.google.com.tr/books?id=4n9AiZtPq5YC.

Hardin, R. (2009). Deliberative Democracy. In T. Christiano & J. Christman (Eds.), *Contemporary debates in political philosophy.* West-Sussex: Blackwell.

Held, D. (2006). *Models of democracy* (3rd ed.). Stanford: Stanford University Press.

Madison, J. (1787). Federalist 10. *The Federalist Papers,* no. 10 (pp. 1–7). http://www.brucesabin.com/pdf_files/readings/Federalist_10.pdf.

Manin, B. (1997). *The principles of representative government.* Cambridge: Cambridge University Press. http://www.cambridge. org/us/academic/subjects/politics-international-relations/political- theory/principles-representative-government.

Mill, J. S. (1859). *On liberty.* Kitchener: Batoche. http://www. amazon.com/Liberty-Dover-Thrift-Editions/dp/0486421309/ref=la_B000APZ4H4_1_1?s=books&ie=UTF8&qid=1400687071&sr= 1-1, http://books.google.com/books?hl=en&lr=&id=LIRp0mUrlsM C&oi=fnd&pg=PA7&dq=On?Liberty&ots=hwSXQSCwNp&sig= QMROngY-5koGwMeDVg9-y8YGa0.

Mitchell, A., Gottfried, J., Kiley, J., & Matsa, K. (2014). *Political polarization & media habits.* http://www.journalism.org/files/ 2014/10/Political-polarization-and-Media-Habits-FINAL-REPORT-11-10-14-2.pdf.

Mouffe, C. (1999). Deliberative democracy or agonistic pluralism? *Social Research,* 66(3), 745–758.

Mouffe, C. (2009). *The democratic paradox.* London: Verso.

Pettit, P. (1999). *Republicanism: A theory of freedom and government.* Oxford: Oxford University Pres.

Rawls, J. (1971). *A theory of justice.* Harvard: Harvard University Press.

Rawls, J. (1997). The idea of public reason. In J. Bohman & W. Rehg (Eds.), *Deliberative democracy: Essays on reason and politics* (p. 447). Cambridge: MIT Press.

Sunstein, C. R. (2007). *Republic.com 2.0.* First Edit. Princeton: Princeton University Press.

Talisse, R. B. (2005). Deliberativist responses to activist challenges: A continuation of Young's dialectic. *Philosophy & Social Criticism,.* doi:10.1177/0191453705052978.

Young, I. M. (2002). *Inclusion and democracy (Oxford political theory).* Oxford: Oxford University Press.

Periodical and Internet Sources Bibliography

Sally Adee, "Keeping Up E-ppearances: How to Bury Your Digital Dirt." *New Scientist*, February 16, 2011. https://www.newscientist.com/article/mg20928001-600-keeping-up-e-ppearances-how-to-bury-your-digital-dirt

Jacob Brogan, "The Relationship Between Social Media and Organ Donation? It's Complicated," Slate, May 19, 2017. http://www.slate.com/articles/technology/future_tense/2017/05/give_and_live_hopes_to_make_living_organ_donation_less_complicated.html

John Degen, "Filter Bubbles and Fake News. How Free Is Our Individual Expression on the Internet?" Centre for Free Expression, November 30, 2016. https://www.cfe.ryerson.ca/blog/2016/11/filter-bubbles-and-fake-news-how-free-our-individual-expression-internet.

Cory Doctorow, "Feds Admit They Used Secret Anti-Terror Mass Surveillance Tool to Catch an Undocumented Waiter," Boing Boing, May 19, 2017. http://boingboing.net/2017/05/19/swatting-jaywalkers-with-tacti.html.

Cory Doctorow, "UK Tories Say They'll Exploit Manchester's Dead to Ban Working Crypto in the UK," Boing Boing, May 24, 2017. https://boingboing.net/2017/05/24/tories-vs-technology.html.

Darren Laur, Social Media Camp, 2017. https://socialmediacamp.ca/history/social-media-camp-victoria-2011/speakers/featured-speakers/darren-laur.

Josephine Livingstone, "The First Great Instagram Novel," *New Republic*, March 17, 2017. https://newrepublic.com/article/141399/first-great-instagram-novel.

New Scientist, "How to Build a Good Reputation Online." February 16, 2011. https://www.newscientist.com/article/mg20928002-900-how-to-build-a-good-reputation-online.

Annie Murphy Paul, "Why Schools' Efforts to Block the Internet Are So Laughably Lame." Slate, July 1, 2014. http://www.slate.com/articles/technology/future_tense/2014/07/banned_website_awareness_day_why_schools_efforts_to_block_the_internet_are.html.

"Research Guides for JSTOR." JSTOR, updated May 2017. http://guides.jstor.org/?cid=soc_tw_JSTOR.

OPPOSING
VIEWPOINTS®
SERIES

CHAPTER 2

How Do Online Filter Bubbles Affect the Information We Consume?

Chapter Preface

Online news aggregators and social media sites and search engines provide readers with news as well as research personalized to suit individual interests. Personalization of news allows us to stay informed about the issues we care about, but we're missing out on all kinds of important stories because of aggregators.

Mark Zuckerberg, founder and CEO of Facebook, is famously quoted as saying that we know more about the dead squirrel in our yard than we know about people dying in Africa. The news we get online can be *too* personalized, meeting the interests of readers but not serving their need to know about other important issues.

To an extent, we have always been manipulated by the media. News organizations have their own agendas, no matter how unbiased they strive to be, and seek out certain stories. Advertisers and editorial boards have sway over the information we receive. But because of online filters, we are manipulated to an even greater extent. For instance, it has been determined that the 2016 US presidential election was manipulated by online filters.

How will online filter bubbles eventually affect the news sources themselves? Perhaps some will thrive because of personalization, even if they haven't worked to deserve it. Others may wither away because of lack of attention or revenue because they are done in by the process of filtering. Some personalities and networks are revealing themselves to be producing reliably sincere journalism and research; others are not.

> *"The most basic impact of filtering is that it reduces visibility of information in your streams."*

We Can Burst Our Own Filter Bubbles

Sidharth Sreekumar

In the following viewpoint, Sidharth Sreekumar expresses the opinion that, while social media content lulls us into a reassuring, reinforcing bubble, people can take action to access information from outside their own small circles of acquaintance. An open mind and a willingness to verify information are the first steps. Online filter bubbles are not just occurring in the United States, the author argues; breaking filter bubbles can be equally important to citizens around the world. Sreejumar writes for the Wire *and is product innovation manager for The Smart Cube, a business-to-business development company.*

As you read, consider the following questions:

1. What is a worrying trend in India, according to the author?
2. What is information blinkering?
3. How can people make up for being vulnerable to manipulation?

"NotMyFilter: Bursting Our Own Filter Bubbles to Save Democracy," by Sidharth Sreekumar, the *Wire*, November 21, 2016. Reprinted by permission.

NotMyPresident" screamed placards just a day after Donald Trump swept the polls to unexpectedly win the US presidential election. The operative word here, "unexpectedly."

Just consider this—towards the end of October when news surfaced that an AI system called MogIA was pipping Trump for victory, most people ignored it as the media and polls told them otherwise. Had they paid a bit more attention they would have realised that the system was probably the closest thing they could have gotten to an unbiased opinion.

The system—which had been built to develop its own rules instead of relying on algorithms written by developers who themselves might suffer from biases – was assessing over 20 million data points from various online platforms such as Google, YouTube and Twitter. In the process, it cut across party lines to come up with its unbiased prediction. Yet large swathes of the Clinton camp had genuinely believed for months now that victory was theirs, only to be blindsided in the end by a result no one saw coming.

At least not in their *filter bubble*.

Not Only an American Problem

This obliviousness is a critical threat posed by filter bubbles created by social media algorithms. Their algorithms identify the kind of stories and sources you and your friends like, and try to show you more of the same. The end effect is a closed confine of comforting and relatable news—a filter bubble. The continuous filtering envelops you in a cocoon of reassuring and familiar news stories and information, and eventually locks you within a proverbial echo chamber where you only end up only receiving material that conforms with your sensibilities.

These bubbles can be directly linked to the increasingly polarised debates across the globe. Even in India there has been a worrying trend of late to label everything neatly as right or left. Dissenting views from one's own are easily labelled as "Aaptards," "Sanghis," "Khangressi" and so on.

WHAT TO DO WHEN YOUR FEED BECOMES AN ECHO CHAMBER

At the outset, the Internet was expected to be an open, democratic source of information. But algorithms, like the kind used by Facebook, instead often steer us toward articles that reflect our own ideological preferences, and search results usually echo what we already know and like.

As a result, we aren't exposed to other ideas and viewpoints, says Eli Pariser, CEO of Upworthy, a liberal news website. Pariser tells NPR's Elise Hu that as websites get to know our interests better, they also get better at serving up the content that reinforces those interests, while also filtering out those things we generally don't like.

"What most algorithms are trying to do is to increase engagement, increase the amount of attention you're spending on that platform," he says. And while it's a nice that we have an instrument to help us cope with the fire hose of information supplied by the Internet, that algorithm also carries some downsides. "The danger is that increasingly you end up not seeing what people who think differently see and in fact not even knowing that it exists."

It's what Pariser calls a "filter bubble." And it's something he tried to break out of himself, chronicling that experience in the book *The Filter Bubble: What the Internet Is Hiding from You.* The results were, well, mixed.

"I was medium successful," Pariser says. "It's hard, and that's partly because we know the people that we know, and those tend to be slanted in one ideological direction or another so you have to really work to find people who think differently."

The difficulty of bursting this filter bubble extends to matters of race too, as NPR's Gene Demby noted in an interview with *Weekend Edition*.

"When you see poll numbers about the vast space between the way people of color feel about policing—or any number of issues around equality—and where white people stand on those issues, it can be explained in part by the fact that we are not having the same conversations," Demby said...

"You would think that social media would bridge a bunch of divides, right?" Demby said. "But maybe the ideal way these conversations need to happen is one-on-one with people who are equally vested in the relationship between the two people."

"The Reason Your Feed Became an Echo Chamber—And What to Do About It," NPR, July 24, 2016.

While it is easy to just blame it on politics, we can't deny the underlying impact of computer algorithms, which themselves view everything in the binary, thus washing away the grey areas of our public discourse.

The overall impact of such filtering can be broken down into the following effects, which both individually and cumulatively shape public discourse.

- Information blinkering: The most basic impact of filtering is that it reduces visibility of information in your streams. You get digital "blinkers" slapped onto you thereby restricting your field of vision to only what the algorithms decide is right for you.
- Entrenching biases: As this information tends to be generally viewpoints you agree with or believe (decided by the fact that you like, read and share them) the algorithms encode your tastes that much deeper. Eventually you will end up only receiving material that conforms with your sensibilities, locking you in a proverbial echo chamber and entrenching your existing biases.
- Rationalising fears: The filter shock when you step out of your bubble can be disorienting. This disorientation can make opinions and views seemingly different than one's own seem alien and alarming, thereby feeding into the fear psychosis of all that is outside the bubble.
- Opinion entitlement: Repeated bombardment of similar opinions and views helps solidify feelings into "facts", thereby

making it easier to waive off any differing views that might occasionally crop up in our feeds. It also aids normalising more extreme views due to continuous affirmation from a similar thinking network. No wonder Oxford dictionary's word of the year is "post-truth."

- Discourse divide: The final and the most critical impact that derives from all of the above is building chasm in public discourse, as the algorithms drive diverging views into their own sealed off bubbles. Just ask the British who realised after their momentous vote that their public was effectively voting on completely different agendas.

Bursting Our Own Bubble

While things have not yet reached an impasse in India (I'm glad I'm still able to debate issues with friends without melodrama), it isn't hard to see that we're sitting on a ticking time bomb. There is already growing clamour for platforms such as Facebook to put stricter content guidelines in place. However, experiments with this in the past have been more worrying than relieving. Given the complex nature of these platforms and the intricate nature of debate around content monitoring, it will be a while before any proper solution emerges.

In the meanwhile, is our social discourse and, by extension, our very democratic principles under threat? Probably, but that doesn't mean there aren't measures a discerning reader can take to burst their own bubble.

They can consume news across the spectrum. One of the key drawbacks of consuming news on social platforms is that they tend to provide you pieces only from your most frequented sources. Over time this tends to enclose you in a bubble. The best way out is to consistently search for varied and even contradicting sources, thereby ensuring that you are at least listening to all sides of an argument.

The reader must also understand the importance of verification. In an age where opinions are coming to matter more than facts, it is the responsibility of each individual to ensure that they are not propagating fallacies. This also helps ensure your news feed does not get populated with dodgy sources. With all sides of the spectrum readily promoting half-truths and even outright lies to suit their narrative, it has become imperative to fact-check as much as possible. The simplest (but not fool-proof) way to do this, is to do just a quick Google search to see if other "reputable" publications are also reporting the same. If not, don't click that share button!

Focusing on facts instead of opinion might also help. This is a contentious point, but still one worth considering. With the large amount of rhetoric and exaggeration floating around in the social sphere, it might be best to focus more on facts. Opinions by their very nature, appeal to our emotions and are hence more difficult to judge. While trying to avoid opinions altogether might be an exercise in futility, a more weighted focus on facts might at the very least steer us clear of gross fallacies. [Note: Sprinkle this point with a heavy dose of Google search.]

Finally, wrapped in our comfort streams, it can often be a shock for us to hear someone articulate something completely contradictory to our beliefs. While our instant reaction might be one of disbelief and even ridicule, we need to consistently strive to be open to new ideas and opinions. After all as Thomas Jefferson put it, the cornerstone of democracy rests on the foundation of an educated (unbiased) electorate.

While these measures might sound like a lot of work—and they probably are—it is still worth the effort to avoid the mass polarisation and political detachment we have seen elsewhere. #NotMyFilter

> *"It is dispiriting seeing a false claim garner thousands of retweets while the separate correction collects only 20 or so."*

Misinformation Was Widely Circulated During the 2016 Presidential Election

Claire Wardle

In the following viewpoint, Claire Wardle argues that it is all too easy to circulate misinformation. The author uses the 2016 election season to illustrate the most widespread types of misinformation. Some examples she cites are stories that are completely made up from start to finish; real images that have been pasted together to make a fake one; and even stories that use a small fact out of context to construct a bigger and more dangerous lie. The author also examines who is telling these fake news stories and how readers can spot the fakes instead of falling for the lies. Wardle is the research director of the Tow Center for Digital Journalism and the cofounder of Eyewitness Media Hub.

"6 Types of Misinformation Circulated This Election Season," by Claire Wardle, *Columbia Journalism Review*, November 18, 2016. Reprinted by permission.

As you read, consider the following questions:

1. How can an editor manage information so that fewer deliberate lies are published?
2. Why is spam a good comparison when it comes to fake news?
3. What is parody content?

F ake news isn't new. Think back to Hurricane Sandy four years ago, when incredible amounts of false content circulated, including claims the NYSE was flooded and sharks appeared on flooded streets in New Jersey. At the time, there was much debate about how to deal with these issues. *The New Yorker's* Sasha Frere-Jones called Twitter a "self-cleaning oven," suggesting that false information could be flagged and self-corrected almost immediately. We no longer had to wait 24 hours for a newspaper to issue a correction.

Post presidential election, we are reckoning with the scale of misinformation circulating online, enabled by social platforms such as Facebook and Twitter. As we look to fix our broken information ecosystem, the most frequent suggestion is platforms should hire hundreds of editors who work in multiple languages and decide what should or should not be seen. But, as Jeff Jarvis wrote over the weekend, we need to be careful what we wish for: We don't want Facebook to become the arbiter of truth.

Instead, I would encourage the social platforms to include prominent features for filtering and flagging. They should work with journalists and social psychologists to invent a new visual grammar so that when content is fact-checked, debunked, corrected, or verified, those processes are transparent and available to anyone seeking to understand more about the origins of a story.

One way this could work in the form of a watermark, embedded with the original piece of content. It is dispiriting seeing a false claim garner thousands of retweets while the separate correction collects only 20 or so. These watermarks would work like a spam filter, making it more likely I would see authenticated content on my feed rather than fake content. Some fake content might slip through, and some authentic content might be marked as "spam," but like my email inbox, I'll take the imperfections if it improves my access to information.

We have much bigger problems than just the fake news sites circulating on Facebook—this is a concern for news organizations using social media to discover content, as well. To begin to develop a grammar of fake news, I collected six types of false information we've seen this election season.

1. Authentic Material Used in the Wrong Context

Donald Trump's first campaign ad purported to show migrants crossing the border from Mexico, when the footage was actually migrants crossing from Morocco to Melilla in North Africa. This content isn't fake, but the context is wrong.

In the weeks leading up the election, a video emerged that appeared to show ballot-box stuffing. As Alastair Reid from First Draft News, of which I am a member, explained, the date stamp in the top left hand corner shows it was captured on September 18, the date of elections in Russia. A quick Google reverse image search also confirms the origin of the footage. Again, the content isn't fake, the context is wrong.

2. Imposter News Sites Designed to Look Like Brands We Already Know

Eric Trump and campaign spokesperson Kellyanne Conway both retweeted [an article from a] fake ABC news site:

If you look closely at the URL, you see it's abc.com.co, which is not an official ABC News domain. *The New York Times* and *Daily Mail* have also recently been copied. Clone Zone is a site that makes this incredibly easy to do.

NowThis was also the victim of a hoax; someone used NowThis branding to create a fake video in early October. Because NowThis publishes entirely on social media and does not have a destination website, it corrected this perception on the social web. As more brands live in a purely distributed environment, the social networks have a responsibility to find a way for corrections to travel with content.

3. Fake News Sites

Out of all these types of misleading content, fake news sites have been subject to the most scrutiny since the election. Work by BuzzFeed journalist Craig Silverman over the past few weeks has highlighted Macedonian teenagers creating fake news articles purely to make money. His most recent analysis shows how much engagement fake news articles gathered on Facebook.

The infamous Pope endorsement [of Donald Trump] story originated on WTOE 5 News, which describes itself as a "fantasy news site" on its "About" page—one click too many for most users. There should be ways to flag such sites that are blatantly creating fake stories.

Brian Forde, a researcher at MIT, recently compared fake news with email spam. We accept the need for junk folders despite occasionally losing "good" emails, he said, because the alternative is drowning in a sea of spam. It seems that social media users would benefit from some automated process that mark sources as fake. If users ever want to dive into that junk feed they can, but they probably won't.

4. Fake Information

Besides fake news sites, fake information is also frequently presented in graphics, images, and video. Designed to be highly shareable, these memes fill up newsfeeds and are often so creative and convincing in their delivery that most users do not think to question their authenticity, let alone know how or where to start checking.

[I]mages were circulating online just before the US election, incorrectly claiming people could stay at home and vote via text.

5. Manipulated Content

Images and videos that have been deliberately manipulated are a huge part of the news ecosystem. Because they can be created easily by bedroom hoaxers, they are often trivialized and dismissed as merely mischievous. But just as prank calls are no longer funny when made to an emergency service, photoshopped hoaxes are no longer harmless when they relate to an election, terror attack, or humanitarian crisis.

[One] photograph surfaced online a couple of weeks before the US election and appears to show an ICE official making an arrest at a voting station.

A simple reverse image search shows that the two men were edited into the original photograph, which was actually taken in Arizona during the primaries in March. Again, this example highlights the importance of finding a way for corrections to travel with fake content. Expecting every user to perform the same verification checks is not realistic or efficient.

6. Parody Content

Parody content makes it hard to think about creating algorithmically driven rules to label fake content. (Although, it would certainly be possible to create a database of satirical sites all over the world. This might even help people who fall for The Onion.)

When Chuck Todd interviewed Rudy Giuliani on *Meet the Press*, he pushed Giuliani about a tweet he had sent in reference to the first debate.

When Giuliani made it clear he hadn't tweeted this, Todd was forced to explain to viewers that the tweet had actually come from a parody account, which describes itself as a pastiche of the former mayor in its bio.

> "*Eliminating fake news won't change the fact that voters ignore ideas contrary to their beliefs.*"

Filter Bubbles Are Not the Media's Real Problem

Bharat N. Anand

In the following viewpoint, Bharat N. Anand examines the US media in the wake of the 2016 presidential campaign. Amid criticisms of bias and sensationalism many have blamed fake news and online filter bubbles for the outcome of the election. But the real problem, the author argues, is the shift in content delivery. Gone are the days when mass media had a monopoly on news coverage. With the advent of online sources and social media, an intense competition has arisen. Traditional news outlets are forced to follow sensational stories to achieve ratings and generate dollars. Anand is the Henry R. Byers Professor of Business Administration in the strategy unit at Harvard Business School and writes for Harvard Business Review.

As you read, consider the following questions:

1. What difference does it make which news agency is reporting a story?
2. Do most readers disagree with people's opinions because of facts or beliefs?
3. How do social media users become the marketing workers for a campaign?

The U.S. media has come under intense scrutiny, with analysts, politicians, and even journalists themselves accusing it of bias and sensationalism—of having failed us—in its coverage of the presidential election. Critics across the political spectrum have said that fake news and cyberattacks played a big role in determining the course of events. The prevailing logic has an "if only" tenor: *If only* the media had been less swayed by shocking stories, *if only* bias in the media had been purged, and *if only* fake news had been eliminated and cyberattacks curtailed, the outcome would have been different. The presidential transition has been marked by the same attitude: *if only* the media were less distractible and headlines more accurate.

Thinking that way is tempting, but it misses the mark. The media did exactly what it was designed to do, given the incentives that govern it. It's not that the media sets out to be sensationalist; its business model leads it in that direction. Charges of bias don't make the bias real; it often lies in the eye of the beholder. Fake news and cyberattacks are triggers, not causes. The issues that confront us are structural.

To the question, *If the media were to cover the election again, with the benefit of hindsight, could we expect anything different?* my answer is a sobering no. This is for two reasons: the way news is produced and amplified (the supply side) and the way consumers process news (the demand side).

A caveat is in order. The analysis here is not concerned with which candidate deserved to win or whose message was "better."

It is concerned with examining the media and its coverage, identifying its root causes, and understanding what we should expect going forward.

The Supply Side I: Connectedness Matters More than Content or Money

Political campaigns are marketing campaigns, messages aimed at selling a product. Like marketers, politicians obsess over messaging (what journalists would call "content") and a few key metrics that historically have determined success: amount of television advertising, number of "foot soldiers," intensity of get-out-the-vote operations, and voter demographics. But in the last two contests in which Hillary Clinton has participated, the 2008 primary and the 2016 election, she won on most of these metrics—and lost the elections.

Two developments bear noting. First, and most obvious, traditional media is no longer the only way to spread the word. Any candidate can communicate directly and instantly with millions of people. Media companies are experiencing an extreme form of competition that comes with digital technologies: Everyone is a media company today.

Second, and even more significant, social media is distinct from traditional media in that it connects users to each other. This means that messages can spread far more easily and quickly (compare how often you share a TV ad and a tweet).

The implications are threefold:

The best product doesn't always win

Even if you have the best product or candidate, if you run a hub-and-spokes campaign, you'll attract followers one by one. Create a product or candidate that connects users, and your message—and advantage—will spread rapidly. Apple learned this the hard way. For 20 years, starting in 1984, the Macintosh was superior to any PC. Yet by 2004 its market share was down to 3%. Apple had a great product, but Microsoft had a network of connected users. Because more people used PCs, and wrote software for them, they became the default choice for nearly everyone.

Many organizations and entrepreneurs miss this lesson. Focus only on creating the best content or product, and you can lose because of untapped user connections—a phenomenon I call the "content trap." It explains why firms that have anchored their strategies to content have ceded digital leadership to those that have focused on connections.

Consider the Scandinavian media firm Schibsted, which engineered an impressive digital transformation through a philosophy of connectedness. It focused its efforts on earning a majority share of Europe's digital classified advertising market (a product that connects buyers and sellers). It then shifted its news focus from great content to content rooted in the question "Can we help readers help each other?" During the volcanic ash crisis of 2010, what it offered wasn't prize-winning stories about the roots of the eruption or its health implications, but an app (Hitchhiker's Central) that allowed readers to share travel plans and offer rides to each other. Similarly, during the 2016 election, many American voters found journalistic content less relevant than what they were experiencing in their own lives.

Bigger marketing budgets may not pay off

In a digital world full of product clutter, the best marketing campaigns spend nearly nothing. JC Penney spent no money on television advertising during the 2015 Super Bowl, yet its "mittens" campaign was one of the most watched. The campaign relied solely on Twitter and went viral by virtue of intentional spelling mistakes. Once a "connected" product draws in users, those users effectively become the sales force. Facebook, Uber, and Airbnb are all examples of this. Donald Trump spent only half of what Clinton did during the campaign.

Expectations matter

In connected worlds, expectations about future growth affect what current users choose; people want to be on a winning platform. This has led to a strategy known as *vaporware*, a term for when firms announce strengths they may not possess or supposedly imminent product launches to draw users. Consider Trump's first words in the June 2015 announcement of his candidacy: "Wow. Whoa. That is some group of people. Thousands....This is beyond anybody's expectations. There's been no crowd like this." This wasn't just a campaign message; it was an effort to shape expectations and trigger connectedness.

The Supply Side II: Ratings Determine Which Messages Get Amplified

The first phase of a marketing campaign is deciding how and where to spend your marketing dollars. The second is influencing how your message gets amplified. One of the most important mechanisms for this is traditional media—so-called "earned media coverage." You can spend a lot in the first phase and get little amplification in the second, or vice versa.

Recycling the same message won't earn amplification. And in today's media environment, even "normal" news doesn't break through information clutter; big, surprising events do. The media's bias toward big events stems from three features of its economics:

Fixed costs

The cost of covering a golf tournament doesn't depend on whether Tiger Woods plays. But if he does, ratings—and revenue—double. The same phenomenon affects decisions about covering news stories or political rallies.

An advertising-based model

Advertising (and other indirect charges like cable operator fees) are central to the economics of most news media, and this creates a bias whereby the number of viewers is more important than whether viewers like the coverage. (What matters is that you watch news coverage, not whether you are ready to throw a chair at it out of disgust.) Fixed costs have always been central to the economics of media. Advertising came later—and when it did, in the early 20th century, news became more sensational. That's hardly surprising: The main metric by which news outlets are judged is the ratings they command, the page views they get, or the copies they sell.

Spillovers

A big event in media and entertainment doesn't just draw viewers to the event itself; it also entices viewers to consume follow-on or related products (and a company's previous products, too). People who watch a television program are far more likely to watch the next program on that channel, for example.

Each of these factors, individually, means that ratings or page views—the size of the audience—matter a lot for media firms. Together, they lead to a fixation on ratings to the exclusion of almost anything else. Competition further reinforces this dynamic, making audience size *the* metric by which media firms are measured. The outcome is a "ratings bubble" within which companies operate.

Big-event bias is even more pronounced in entertainment worlds, where getting noticed has gotten increasingly hard over time. This explains the trend toward spinoffs, sequels, and franchises in broadcast television and movies (viewers are already familiar with the basic story) and big-name authors in books (they generate publicity) and why successful sports franchises tend to get even more successful over time (they draw lots of viewers, which allows them to spend more on star players, who draw even more viewers). Success might have more to do with awareness than with quality. When the pseudonymous Robert Galbraith published *A Cuckoo's Calling* in 2013, the novel sold about 1,500 copies in the first month. After the author was revealed to be Harry Potter creator J.K. Rowling, sales rose to over one million.

Piggybacking on big events has allowed certain media companies to grow over time. Fox News, for instance, entered the seemingly mature cable market in 1996 and experienced notable upticks in viewers after "big news" events—the 2000 election, the 9/11 terrorist attacks, and the start of the war in Iraq. When an event drew viewers to cable news in general, Fox's ratings grew along with the other networks'. But more of the viewers who tuned into Fox stayed with it *after* the event had passed when they realized the network's coverage was different.

In political campaigns, big events arise in one of three ways. The first is sporadically and unpredictably, as with the San Bernardino shooting or the *Access Hollywood* tape. The timing of such surprises can be particularly fortuitous or damaging (see: James Comey). The second is through name recognition. Events become more newsworthy if they're accompanied by a big name. The third is by being created. Steve Jobs understood this more than most technology executives, which is why he elevated product launches to an art form: Every media firm *had* to cover a new Apple release. And Trump understood this more than any other candidate: Every time he made a provocative comment on a new subject, the news outlets covered it.

These forces help explain why Trump got so much more media coverage than, say, Bernie Sanders, who touted a similarly antiestablishment, populist message. Populism and inequality aren't news; calling Mexican immigrants rapists and vowing to build a wall are. So Sanders's brand of populism wasn't news; Trump's was. The reason was rooted in media economics, not in the effort or preferences of journalists and programming executives. A combination of fixed costs, an advertising-reliant model, and spillovers produced a staggering difference in earned media coverage during the primaries: $2 billion for Trump and $300 million for Sanders. Television advertising, where Clinton had a huge leg up on both, hardly seemed to matter at all.

Competition Can Backfire

Competition and private firms operating in their self-interest typically lead to well-functioning markets. But that's not always what happens. A well-known exception occurs when externalities exist—side effects on other people or firms that aren't usually accounted for by private actors. (Canonical examples are cigarette smoking or pollution, or a store manager in a large retail chain pursuing actions that benefit his individual store but damage the parent company's brand.) In situations like these, following your self-interest (in this case, as a media firm) doesn't necessarily further the collective good, or even your own.

In 2009 Netflix needed high-quality content to grow its streaming business. It could get that content only from Hollywood studios. The studios had seen Netflix grow its DVD business for a decade, and now, with a stronger bargaining position in the streaming market—the first-sale doctrine that allowed any DVD owner to resell did not apply to streaming—they could have chosen not to license to Netflix and nipped it in the bud. But they granted licenses, and Netflix soon became the giant they hadn't wanted to see arise. Why did the studios act against their own interests?

If they could have collectively agreed not to license to Netflix, the result would have been different. But they couldn't. At first only Viacom relented, licensing archived *Beavis and Butt-head* episodes. One show, it reasoned, could not a streaming giant make. But then everyone followed that logic.

It wasn't that the content providers didn't see what was happening; it was that they couldn't coordinate. It's why newspapers let Google crawl their content for Google News. It's why they handed content to Facebook for its Instant Articles format last year.

So, too, with the recent political campaign. If every media outlet had ignored Trump's rallies and rhetoric, it would have paid handsomely for one outlet to cover them. But once one *did* cover them, no others could afford not to.

These events coalesced dramatically toward the end of the campaign, when Trump announced a press conference in which he would ostensibly make a major announcement about President Obama's birth certificate (a lie that he had prolonged that had found traction in media coverage several years back). Nearly every media outlet showed up. How could they not cover a major announcement by a presidential candidate? But it was a sham—there was no real announcement, other than that there would be no more announcements on the subject.

This is the prisoner's dilemma of reporting amid competition: Following your self-interest does not always further the collective good. The situation generated one of the most dispiritingly candid statements ever from a media executive: Early in 2016, when the head of CBS was asked about the disproportionate attention given to Trump, he quipped, "It may not be good for America, but it's damn good for CBS."

The network wasn't alone. Cable news outlets enjoyed similar gains in 2016, marking it as their best year ever. Meanwhile, public trust in the press reached its lowest level in history.

The Demand Side: Consumers Consume What They Want To

One of the longest-standing debates in marketing is not *whether* advertising works, but *how* it does. One view is that marketing persuades consumers to purchase. Hear a song once, and you may not like it; hear it repeatedly, and you'll start to, regardless of how good or bad it is (hence the phrase "all publicity is good publicity"). Others argue that marketing merely increases awareness without altering beliefs. By this reasoning, repeated exposure to a song that doesn't match your taste might make you *less* likely to buy it.

Does media reporting change what we believe, or do our preferences shape what media we choose to watch in the first place?

Most research indicates that the latter is central: Our preexisting preferences largely determine what media we watch. One of the most reliable findings in the study of television entertainment is that viewers watch programs whose characters are like themselves. Older people watch shows featuring older characters, younger viewers watch shows featuring younger ones; the same goes for gender, ethnicity, and income. A similar effect is seen in news: We watch outlets whose reporting is consistent with our beliefs. Viewers who identify with the right are more likely to watch Fox, while left-leaning people are more likely to watch MSNBC. Similar differences apply to intra-network program choices, since programs on the same network can differ in their positioning.

These patterns in news-watching would be puzzling if all that news providers did was provide verifiably objective information. But like entertainment programs, news programs and channels differ in their positioning, in the way they report information (often referred to as *slant*), and in what information they report (*agenda setting*). News positioning matters—viewers watch news programs and channels whose positions match their tastes and beliefs.

This pattern of sorting on beliefs is amplified over time by various additional factors. The first is competition among media, which has increased as digital technologies have led to a vast number of new media outlets, each catering to more-niche tastes. The second is viewers' confirmation bias, which leads us to reject valid information that is not consistent with our beliefs. Confirmation bias is deeply rooted in human behavior. It affects not just how we process information but who we associate with, creating "filter bubbles." These bubbles are further reinforced by website algorithms designed to personalize the information we receive based on our past behaviors. Persuasive effects of the media also serve to solidify these bubbles. (And even small persuasive effects can have large effects in close elections.)

Each factor increases viewer polarization, which on certain measures has reached unprecedented levels. Together, they shape how we respond to bias in the media. Consider the debate over left and right media bias, which goes back several decades and has grown in intensity over time. Part of what makes discussions of bias so thorny is that we almost never agree on what bias is. Both the debate and studies tend to focus on what the media reports —on content. But studies show that content is not the only place where bias lives. In experiments, when two people with different beliefs view *exactly the same content*, their perceptions of bias differ.

Add it all up, and the implications are profound.

First, we watch what we believe, but what we *don't* watch, we *don't* believe. This is the effect of sorting based on beliefs.

Second, negative coverage can have unintended consequences. Hear a source you don't trust, and when it reports something inconsistent with your beliefs, you'll discount that thing even more. (The rare exception is when events are incontrovertibly verifiable—for example, the question of who said what on the *Access Hollywood* tape.) During the election season, more newspapers endorsed Clinton than any presidential candidate in U.S history. Papers with a tradition of endorsing Republicans endorsed her; papers with a tradition of not endorsing a candidate did, too. But none of it mattered; editorial content was essentially irrelevant.

Third, and for the same reason, charges of media bias can actually help an outlet. The more your favorite channel is alleged to be biased by people you disagree with, the more you'll watch it. Trump wasn't the first to see this phenomenon: In Fox News's early days, senior executives often acknowledged that charges of bias appeared to help them. And it isn't specific to right-leaning voters. After the election, when Trump tweeted complaints about the New York Times and Vanity Fair, both outlets saw a rise in subscriptions. Charges of bias harden beliefs and reinforce polarization.

Particularly sobering is that all this has nothing do with the much-lamented problem of fake news. Get rid of all verifiably fake news, as Facebook and others certainly should, and filter bubbles, polarization, and charges of media bias will remain.

Where Does This Leave Us?

Three forces combine to create the media coverage of political campaigns we observe today: connected media, which spreads messages faster than traditional media; fixed costs and advertising-reliant business models in traditional media, which amplify sensational messages; and viewers' news consumption patterns, which leads to people sorting across media outlets based on their beliefs and makes messages they already agree with far more effective. Each reinforces the others. Without these enabling factors, even the best marketing campaign would go nowhere, and fake news or leaked information from cyberattacks would have little effect.

Fair questions have been raised about the lack of investigative journalism early in the campaign, false equivalencies in reporting, and the use of paid campaign operatives as experts on television news. But digital technology and business incentives exerted more influence over the media coverage than editorial decisions and missing voices did. The ratings bubble had as much impact as filter bubbles did. The forces at work here—the search for profitability, competition, and self-interest—are things we embrace as profoundly American.

Competition in the media leads to efficiency as well as to checks and balances—all good things. But it fails to internalize the externalities from profitable but sensational coverage. It leads to differentiation and more voices (also good, and what's been the focus of regulatory efforts) but also to fragmentation, polarization, and less-penetrable filter bubbles (dangerous).

It's tempting to stretch the analysis between marketing and politics too far. They are different in important respects. Most notable, in marketing you can win through strategies that exploit the big-event bias of media (through attention-grabbing rhetoric) and the beliefs of consumers (through allegations that discredit your competitors). These strategies draw in consumers who are right for your brand. But in presidential politics, the same approach is incredibly risky because when you win, you serve everyone, not just those who "purchased your product." Despite these differences, the same economics of information supply-and-demand that shape digital strategies in business are doing so in politics.

Which leads to my conclusion: Even if we could somehow push "reset," we would have to expect the same sort of coverage that we got. The problems are too deep and structural for anything else.

What's the way forward? There are no easy answers to the question. This analysis mainly points to solutions that *won't* work. Voluntary efforts at restraint by well-meaning journalists won't work, because of advertising-based business models and competition. Eliminating fake news won't change the fact that voters ignore ideas contrary to their beliefs. And it won't solve the media's structural challenges or change its incentives. Media companies, their regulators, and their customers—all of us—have to look for ways to confront these challenges. The stakes could not be higher.

> *"Instead of creating an ideal type of a digitally mediated 'public agora,' which would allow citizens to voice their concerns and share their hopes, the internet has actually increased conflict and ideological segregation between opposing views."*

The Internet Fuels Conflict and Threatens Democracy

Vyacheslav Polonski

In the following viewpoint, Vyacheslav Polonski examines the internet's democratizing effect. While many once believed the internet would reinforce democracy, since it gives a platform to "the people" to express their views, the result has been quite different. For one, it has allowed marginalized people such as white nationalists to come together and bolster their hateful views. For another, the phenomenon of online filter bubbles serves to fragment and segregate people, in turn disintegrating what philosopher Jean-Jacques Rousseau called the general will of a society. The author warns that policy makers must learn to understand the power of seemingly popular movements rather than reacting to emotional movements. Polonski is a network scientist and a doctoral student in philosophy at the Oxford Internet Institute.

"The Biggest Threat to Democracy? Your Social Media Feed," by Vyacheslav Polonski, World Economic Forum, August 4, 2016. Reprinted by permission.

As you read, consider the following questions:

1. Why should UK politicians have listened to voices on the internet?
2. How has the internet fueled populist ideas?
3. When a minority opinion is not taken as policy, how will a democratic government consider it fairly?

O ver the past two decades, the internet has rewired civil society in unprecedented ways, propelling collective action to a radically new level of citizen autonomy.

Democracy is now not only infrequently exercised at the ballot box, but is lived and experienced online on a day-to-day basis.

Much has been made of the democratizing effect of the internet, and its emancipatory impact on under-represented and marginalized groups living under authoritarian regimes, where it nurtures a networked public sphere that constitutes an independent alternative to tightly controlled media environments.

According to Harvard's Yochai Benkler, this networked public sphere allows for bottom-up agenda-setting, universal access to information, and freedom from governmental interference. Benkler explains: "The various formats of the networked public sphere provide anyone with an outlet to speak, to inquire, to investigate, without need to access the resources of a major media organization."

Since more members of society are now encouraged to participate in public discourse and speak up about matters they deem to be of public concern, the internet has rendered the diversity of citizens' views more salient. This is particularly visible when there is conflict and disagreement between different political or civic interest groups. Whenever there is a controversial policy announcement, there will always be a highly motivated group of people who use the internet to apply enormous pressure on politicians in these moments by voicing their discontent.

Democratic bodies are typically elected in periods of three to five years, yet citizen opinions seem to fluctuate daily and sometimes these mood swings grow to enormous proportions. When thousands of people all start tweeting about the same subject on the same day, you know that something is up. With so much dynamic and salient political diversity in the electorate, how can policy-makers ever reach a consensus that could satisfy everyone? If our representatives are unable to keep up with digital expressions of citizen sentiment, does that mean that we have become ungovernable by the institutions that exist today?

At the same time, it would be a grave mistake to discount the voices of the internet as something that has no connection to real political situations. Last month, British politicians and activists campaigning for Britain to remain in the EU in the recent referendum had to learn this lesson the hard way.

What happened in the UK was not only a political disaster, but also a vivid example of what happens when you combine the uncontrollable power of the internet with a lingering visceral feeling that ordinary people have lost control of the politics that shape their lives. When people feel their democratic representatives do not serve them anymore, they turn to the internet. They look for others who feel the same and moans turn into movements.

In this regard, the Leave campaign's main social media messages appealed to the agency of ordinary voters to reject the rule of the bureaucracy and "take control" of their own country. Using very simple language, largely consisting of only a few syllables, these messages spread very fast across the internet and were often reinforced with amusing memes, instead of rigorous expert opinions or statistics.

Polarization as a Driver of Populism

In light of these recent developments, right-wing populist sentiments have been growing in strength and popularity across both Europe and the US. These movements are fuelled by populist anger, resurgent nationalism, and a deep-rooted hostility towards immigrants.

People who have long entertained right-wing populist ideas, but were never confident enough to voice them openly, are now in a position to connect to like-minded others online and use the internet as a megaphone for their opinions. They become more confident and vigorous, because they see that others share their beliefs. This is concerning, because we know from previous research that increased contact with people who share our views makes our previously held beliefs more extreme. It grants us new group identities that permit us to do things we deemed inconceivable before. In this way, one could argue that the Brexit vote was as much a vote to reclaim one's political independence as it was a vote to reclaim one's lost national identity.

The greater diversity and availability of digital content implies that people may choose to only consume content that matches their own worldviews. We choose who to follow and who to befriend. The resulting echo chambers tend to amplify and reinforce our existing opinions, which is dysfunctional for a healthy democratic discourse. And while social media platforms like Facebook and Twitter generally have the power to expose us to politically diverse opinions, research suggests that the filter bubbles they sometimes create are, in fact, exacerbated by the platforms' personalization algorithms, which are based on our social networks and our previously expressed ideas.

This means that instead of creating an ideal type of a digitally mediated "public agora," which would allow citizens to voice their concerns and share their hopes, the internet has actually increased conflict and ideological segregation between opposing views, granting a disproportionate amount of clout to the most extreme opinions.

The Disintegration of the General Will

In political philosophy, the very idea of democracy is based on the principal of the general will, which was proposed by Jean-Jacques Rousseau in the 18th century. Rousseau envisioned that a society needs to be governed by a democratic body that acts according to the imperative will of the people as a whole.

However, Rousseau foresaw in Book IV of the Social Contract that "when particular interests begin to make themselves felt [...], the common interest changes and finds opponents: opinion is no longer unanimous; the general will ceases to be the will of all; contradictory views and debates arise; and the best advice is not taken without question."

The internet, in particular, intensifies the fragmentation of opinions, allowing people who are most passionate, motivated and outspoken to find likeminded others and make themselves heard—as we have seen on social media in the EU referendum.

In a similar vein, sudden attention-grabbing focusing events, such as natural disasters, terrorist attacks or external shocks to the environment, could also sway public opinion and trigger hasty political decisions with potentially unsustainable repercussions. Politicians run the risk of making important policy-decisions based on current emotional bursts in the population or momentary popular opinions, rather than what is best for the country. For instance, important and far-reaching decisions, such as leaving the EU, would need to be approved by qualified two-thirds majorities in multiple plebiscites over several years.

The critical challenge for policy-makers is, therefore, to learn to distinguish when a seemingly popular movement does actually represent the emerging general will of the majority and when it is merely the echo of a loud, but insignificant minority.

Prospects for a Future-Proof Democracy

There can be no doubt that a new form of digitally mediated politics is a crucial component of the Fourth Industrial Revolution: the internet is already used for bottom-up agenda-setting, empowering citizens to speak up in a networked public sphere, and pushing the boundaries of the size, sophistication and scope of collective action. In particular, social media has changed the nature of political campaigning and will continue to play an important role in future elections and political campaigns around the world.

However, this technology can also be a platform for conflict and malicious agitation by right-wing populists that are dysfunctional for a healthy democratic discourse, while our current governance systems are susceptible to emotional bursts and populist movements that unfold on the internet. What the EU referendum has taught us is that this accelerating technology is open to all and can be used to influence the public agenda in many different ways. Intimated by the power of internet users, our current governance institutions are, however, incapable of handling the dynamism and diversity of digitally-mediated citizen opinions.

We are thus not ungovernable in the long term, but need to govern ourselves in radically new ways. The only way to accomplish that is by re-imagining the institutions that would allow citizens to engage in enlightened debate in an active and inclusive public sphere.

Periodical and Internet Sources Bibliography

Mahsa Alimardani, "What Did Iranian President Rouhani Actually Achieve?" Slate, May 18, 2017. http://www.slate.com/articles/ technology/future_tense/2017/05/did_iranian_president_ rouhani_fulfill_his_campaign_promises.html.

Artstor, "Staying True to the Ethos of Zines at OCAD U," the Artstor Blog, May 17, 2017. https://artstor.wordpress.com/2017/05/17/ staying-true-to-the-ethos-of-zines-at-ocad-u.

Cory Doctorow, "The Filter Bubble: How Personalization Changes Society," BoingBoing, May 23, 2011. http://boingboing. net/2011/05/23/the-filter-bubble-ho.html

Cory Doctorow, "A University Librarian Explains Why Her Zine Collection's Catalog Is Open Access," Boing Boing, May 19, 2017. http://boingboing.net/2017/05/19/ocad-u-zine-library.html.

Dr Nathalia Gjerscoe. "Attention." Brain Bank, January, 2012. http://thebrainbank.org.uk/teaching-materials/brain-function/ attention.

Emily Parker. "Russia Is Trying to Copy China's Approach to Internet Censorship." *New America*, April 6, 2017. https://www. newamerica.org/weekly/edition-160/russia-trying-copy-chinas- approach-internet-censorship.

Seth Stephens-Davidowitz, "Everybody Lies: How Google Search Reveals Our Darkest Secrets," *Guardian*, July 9, 2017. https:// www.theguardian.com/technology/2017/jul/09/everybody- lies-how-google-reveals-darkest-secrets-seth-stephens- davidowitz?CMP=share_btn_tw.

Laura Sydell. "We Tracked Down a Fake-News Creator in the Suburbs. Here's What We Learned." National Public Radio, November 23, 2016. http://www.npr.org/sections/ alltechconsidered/2016/11/23/503146770/npr-finds-the-head-of- a-covert-fake-news-operation-in-the-suburbs.

Dave Weinstein. "To Disclose or Not to Disclose." Slate, May 19, 2017. http://www.slate.com/articles/technology/future_tense/2017/05/ the_process_the_government_uses_to_stockpile_computer_ vulnerabilities_is.html.

How Do Online Filter Bubbles Affect the Choices We Make?

Chapter Preface

Today, many of the more social aspects of our lives are affected by online filters. The personalization of social media can enhance one's life or limit it. Personalization and filtering affect businesses in unexpected ways, changing how people choose to spend money, how they decide to be active in the world, and what sort of homes they make. Students may choose to enter a school and study chosen material filtered for their education.

But do we want someone else curating our life experiences and making choices for us as if we were eternally children? Those curators are not all as benevolent as parents and teachers who mean to help children grow up well and able.

As individuals are affected by filtering, society is being affected in turn. Customs and laws will be affected as time goes on. Public opinions on climate change or vaccination are affected by online filter bubbles, but mentioning one point of view, even to discredit it, keeps it alive in the public awareness. Mentioning two differing points of view just for the sake of balance can make it seem to readers like a fifty-fifty deal, as if half the experts say one idea and the rest believe the other. Sometimes when one point of view saturates a market, that swamping discourages participation in any alternative.

Many internet users caught in online filter bubbles have little or no idea what they are missing out on. It's important to consider who could benefit from people being in online filter bubbles. Savvy users of the internet add variety to their routines, asking themselves "Is online filtering keeping me in a bubble, or am I throwing a monkey wrench into their stack of data?"

> "*The main problem of online search and social media seems to be the drive to personalize results, rather than the networks themselves.*"

Intense Emotions Fuel the Spread of Suspicious Thinking

Kim Mortimer

In the following excerpted viewpoint, Kim Mortimer argues that the main problem of internet searches and social media engagement is the drive to personalize results, not the networks themselves. The author uses results from scientific studies to examine how conspiracy theories flourish online. Conspiracy theories are much more likely to be shared online than neutral posts. As the posts gain "likes" and comments, conspiracy theory discussions are likely to become more negative. But how can the sharing of such dangerous theories be curbed? Censorship is not the answer; in fact, it can end up feeding the theories. The author suggests that encouraging analytical thinking is an effective way to minimize conspiracy theories. Mortimer works in the Dalhousie University School of Information Management in Nova Scotia.

"Understanding Conspiracy Online: Social Media and the Spread of Suspicious Thinking," by Kim Mortimer, *Dalhousie Journal of Interdisciplinary Management*, Spring 2017. https://ojs.library.dal.ca/djim/article/download/6928/6043. Licensed under CC BY 3.0

As you read, consider the following questions:

1. What are some alternative names for conspiracy theories?
2. When people are caught in an echo chamber, what are they missing out on about their favorite topic?
3. Except for those who incite violence or harm, are people really harmed by belief in a conspiracy theory?

The Sharing of Conspiracy

Social media networks allow users to share relevant stories, and offer a window through which researchers can view this sharing. Del Vicario et al. (2016) observed that Facebook posts related to both science and conspiracy topics shared similar "lifetimes"— the time between the original post and the final time the post was shared. However, conspiracy rumors showed a positive correlation between lifetime and how many users were exposed to the rumor: longer lived conspiracies have more impact on social media, validating some of the ideas from Sunstein and Vermeule (2009) on cascades. This common lifetime was also reproduced by Bessi et al. (2015).

Bessi et al. (2015) took a closer look at how posts were commented, liked, and shared on Facebook. There were no significant differences in commenting patterns for conspiracy posts as compared to science posts, but conspiracy posts were more likely to be liked and shared by users (Bessi et al., 2015). Bessi et al. (2016) also studied videos on both Facebook and YouTube and noted science and conspiracy posts have similar user interaction profiles, which were measured by the numbers of likes and comments videos received. These results were replicated by Mocanu et al. (2015). However, Bessi et al. (2015; 2016) and Mocanu et al. (2015) did not study the emotions and sentiments associated with comments in their work, for example, whether particular types of posts were responded to positively or negatively. Sunstein and Vermeule (2009) argued intense emotions have a role in the spread of conspiracy, so understanding the emotions associated with this sharing seems relevant.

Emotions and Sharing

Zollo et al. (2015) used automatic sentiment analysis to attempt to understand the emotional state of users on Facebook who interacted with science and conspiracy pages. Results were divided into comments, posts, and users—users being the aggregate of their comments and posts—and compared for the two communities. They were assigned a rating of positive, neutral or negative. One observation was that the majority of science comments, posts, and users were neutral compared to conspiracy comments, posts and users, which were much more negative. Conspiracy discussions were also more likely to become negative as the number of comments and likes increased (Zollo et al., 2015). This negative background may contribute to feelings of isolation amongst conspiracy theorists. However, no comparison was made to a baseline or control group, that is to say, a group without science or conspiracy discussions.

Polarization and Homogeneity

Bessi and Del Vicario have, across at least three papers (Bessi et al., 2015; Bessi et al., 2016; Del Vicario et al., 2016) used a single definition of polarization: a user's polarization towards conspiracy is the fraction of their interactions (posts, comments, and likes) that are only directed towards conspiracy news. Users who commented frequently on scientific posts were considered to hold a scientific polarization. Polarized users are those with a polarization greater than 95%. Homogeneity is a measure of how similar two sharing users are in their personal polarization—the more similar two users are, the higher the homogeneity (Bessi et al., 2015; Bessi et al., 2016; Del Vicario et al., 2016).

One very interesting result is that most users on Facebook and YouTube are strongly polarized—more than 85% of users studied were either science-polarized or conspiracy-polarized. Users on Facebook were more science-polarized, and on YouTube, users were more conspiracy-polarized. This also shows there are two distinct, isolated communities: one for science and one for conspiracy. Polarized users in the two groups displayed very similar commenting activity; thus, once strongly polarized, users behaved in similar ways despite the differences in content (Bessi et al., 2016). Likes and comments on Facebook were also very similar among polarized groups (Bessi et al., 2015).

Another interesting difference was how science-polarized users commented on conspiracy news, and conspiracy-polarized users commented on scientific news. Conspiracy-polarized users commented roughly ten times less frequently on science news (comprising about ~1% of total polarized comments) when compared to science polarized users commenting on conspiracy news (compromising about ~10% of total polarized comments), even though there were only three times fewer scientific news articles. Conspiracy polarized users were also more likely to comment and like fake or satirical news (Bessi et al., 2015).

Despite this, Del Vicario et al. (2016) noted that conspiracy posts with larger cascades (that is, more success in spreading) generally had a lower homogeneity when compared to science posts. This seems to imply that more successful conspiracy theory posts attract a wider variety of users. Although there was this one particular exception, Del Vicario et al. (2016) state that "homogeneity is clearly the driver of information diffusion" (p. 556) for both science and conspiracy posts.

The Filter Bubble Effect Online

The strong polarization of users who share conspiracy news, combined with the high homogeneity, leads both Del Vicario et al. (2016) and Bessi et al. (2015; 2016) to argue that their results are indicative of echo chambers. Echo chambers and filter bubbles are linked concepts. Filter bubbles generally refer to how a combination of personal preference and learning algorithms for displaying content, such as Facebook's news feed or Google's search personalization, results in users only being exposed to information that aligns with their pre-established beliefs. Thus, an echo chamber forms—sometimes without a user's knowledge (Flaxman, Goel, & Rao, 2016; Messing & Westwood, 2014). The term "filter bubble" originates from Pariser's 2011 book of the same name. Some further analysis of filter bubbles as related to information professionals is provided by Menchaca in his 2012 article, "The future is in doubt," which I discuss in more detail later.

Nyhan (2014) argues that echo chambers do not truly exist in user consumption patterns, noting surveys that show centrist ideologies form a core part of the information diet of respondents. He also hypothesizes that exposure to different ideologies results in a more diverse information diet (Nyhan, 2014). Unsurprisingly, Facebook employees (specifically Bakshy, E., Messing, S., & Adamic, L., 2015) have argued their algorithms are not responsible for the filter bubble effect, but their own studies have shown some conflicting data: some contradictory news stories are removed or hidden from a polarized user's news feed. Its ranking of articles could also create an echo chamber in more subtle ways because the lower the algorithm ranks items, the less likely users are to click on them (Tufekci, 2015).

A variety of studies have attempted to better understand the precise impact of the effect of filter bubbles and echo chambers. Jacobson, Myung, and Johnson (2016) observed that politically inclined users chose sources that agreed with their opinions much more often than those that disagreed with them. However, they also observed that there were a small number of "neutral" resources that were linked to frequently by both left and right leaning users. Unfortunately they did not perform semantic analysis of the links and discussion, leaving it unresolved as to whether these neutral resources were useful to decreasing polarization (Jacobson et al., 2016).

Messing and Westwood (2014) took a closer look at how social media services influence polarization. They observed that users who were shown social endorsements through non-personalized

DOES FACEBOOK KEEP USERS IN POLITICAL BUBBLES?

Facebook's research team focused on the problem of political polarization, asking how much their news feed algorithm contributed. Although the posts scrolling along the site's news feed may seem like a live stream from your friends, the company uses an algorithm to filter out and rank those posts before they reach you. And that algorithm is constantly evolving...

It wasn't hard to determine who the liberals and conservatives were for the study: People can declare their political affiliations on their Facebook profiles. The team mapped those political organizations to a 5-point ideological scale—from –2 for very conservative to +2 for very liberal—based on survey data. After limiting the population to American adults who log in at least 4 days per week, the researchers had just over 10 million test subjects. For content, they focused on news stories.

Determining the political flavor of that content was trickier. Rather than trying to measure the political slant of news stories based on semantic analysis, the team used a far more expedient method: The "political alignment" of each story was determined by the average political alignment of all the users who posted a link to that story. For example, the political alignment score of the average story in *The New York Times* came in at –0.62 (somewhat liberal) whereas the average Fox News story was +0.78 (somewhat conservative). The stories that mattered for this study were the "cross-cutting" ones, news articles with a liberal slant appearing in a conservative person's news feed or vice versa. Armed with all these metrics, the researchers crunched the numbers for every news story—both those that ended up on people's news feeds and those that were filtered out by the algorithm—between 2011 and 2012.

By comparing the two groups of stories, researchers found that Facebook's news feed algorithm does indeed create an echo chamber effect. But it is not as powerful as critics have feared. The algorithm made it only 1% less likely for users to be exposed to politically cross-cutting stories, the team reports online today in *Science*. "The power to expose oneself to perspectives from the other side in social media lies first and foremost with individuals," the team concludes.

"Is Facebook Keeping You in a Political Bubble?" by John Bohannon, AAAS, May 7, 2015.

Facebook "recommendations" were more likely to select non-partisan or contrary sources. Thus, a popular source seems to encourage users to ignore any filtering practices they may have, increasing the diversity of opinions they are exposed to. They claim that this will "make it less likely for individuals to fall victim to falsehoods" (Messing & Westwood, 2014, p. 1058).

Himelboim, McCreery, and Smith (2013) studied how users communicate and share links on Twitter within their networks. They focused on closed clusters of users and observed that clusters grow to reflect the prevailing political opinion; the users thus become more polarized, as hypothesized previously by Sunstein and Vermeule (2009). Polarized clusters were more likely to share ideologically similar links (Himelboim et al., 2013).

Flaxman, Goel, and Rao (2016) offered a comparison between social media networks and online search engines. They observed that both social media and online search generally exposed users to a wider arrange of opinions and opposing viewpoints when compared to news aggregators or directly navigating to a website (Flaxman et al., 2016). Intuitively, this makes some sense, as users who directly navigate to a site are explicitly ignoring other sources. Flaxman et al. (2016) also observed that less polarized users were more likely to consider ideologically challenging sources, reproducing previous effects. They finally measured ideological segregation as the expected difference in polarization between two users of a service, and argued higher segregation indicates a higher likelihood of filter bubbles, in the sense that users of the service are ideologically distinct subsets (Flaxman et al., 2016). This definition reads to me as if a source that attracts a very wide variety of users across the spectrum of polarization will measure a very high segregation, while a source with most users of a particular polarization—whether it is strongly polarized or not —will measure a very low segregation. Thus, a science-focused news source that attracts predominantly science-polarized users would seemingly have a low segregation, despite the implications of the term. They observed that search engines had larger measured segregations as compared to social media or directly navigating to a site (Flaxman et al., 2016).

These diverse studies demonstrate the double-edged sword of the internet. Users are able to form homogenous clusters, and thus form an echo chamber. Equally, the huge amount of sources online, and the ability to see what is popular among other people even people outside your network, offer the opportunity to expose users to heterogeneous sources of information. The main problem of online search and social media seems to be the drive to personalize results, rather than the networks themselves.

Curbing Conspiracy—What Should Be Done?

If we are to challenge conspiracy thinking, what techniques and strategies ought to be used? In some situations, such as the anti-vaccination movement, it seems as if there is a moral imperative to intervene, so as to reduce harm. The spread of factually inaccurate information might also be considered harm. Martin (2015), in reflecting on the anti-vaccination movement in Australia, reported several attempts to curtail the speech of members of the movement. He argues that an intervention in this manner is not only an attempt at censorship, endangering free speech, and offers a series of arguments against any direct legal intervention (Martin, 2015). The WHO appears to agree: Larson, an anthropologist in the employ of the WHO argues that it is better to focus on the underlying individual issues pertaining to anti-vaccination sentiment (Fleck, 2014). If intervention is to be performed, it must be done in such a way that the rights of free speech and free association are not violated. An exception may be necessary in cases of direct incitement to violence or harm.

DeHaven-Smith and Witt (2013) echo some of Martin's (2015) arguments, and criticize Sunstein and Vermeule's (2009) proposal for direct government infiltration of conspiracy theory groups (as included in Sunstein & Vermeule, 2009). "[T]rying to suppress conspiracy theories simply exacerbates citizen disaffection while also undermining the traditional, healthy distrust Americans harbor towards unchecked political power" (deHaven-Smith & Witt, 2013, p. 289). DeHaven-Smith and Witt (2013) instead argue that the concerns of conspiracy theorists be listened to seriously and responded to honestly. They note that previous events that have grown into conspiracy theories, such as the September 11th, 2001 terrorist attacks, generally suffered from various investigative problems, such as loss of evidence or conflicts of interest. Their solution is to develop special procedures guaranteeing timely, comprehensive, objective and independent investigations into major events (deHaven-Smith & Witt, 2013). However, this proposal requires public or government funding to create this independent agency, and must in some way be done without compromising its independence. What about thinking on a smaller scale?

Directly challenging conspiracy theorists on their thinking or beliefs is one possible way for the general public to contribute. Einstein and Glick (2015) noted that users exposed to a conspiracy theory, and then asked whether they believed in it, reported they were less likely to believe in the conspiracy than the control group. They argue that, combined with their other survey results, asking questions acts as a subtle correction to a conspiracy theory (Einstein & Glick, 2015).

Swami, Voracek, Stieger, Tran, & Furnham (2014) observed that by encouraging analytical thinking, belief in conspiracy theories dropped. They offer a variety of possible explanations for this, including the possibility that subjects primed to think analytically merely selected a more rational seeming solution rather than reporting on their true beliefs (Swami et al., 2014). By combining this result with Einstein and Glick's, it may be that users who are challenged directly on their conspiracy beliefs "retreat" from them, perhaps to avoid being seen as "crazy," as noted previously in Harambam's (2015) and Auper's (2012) works. It is also possible that engaging in a critical discourse may encourage analytic thinking and broaden perceptions.

Jong and Dückers (2016) observed in their research a self-correcting effect on Twitter with regards to rumors. In some cases, users were cautious or curious about certain topics and began ad-hoc investigations. The authors suggest that at least some fraction of Twitter users are constantly validating the information they are presented with, and thus participate in correcting the record (Jong & Dückers, 2016). This almost seems like a ray of hope in contrast to the echo bubbles observed previously. One question is whether this "wisdom of crowds" could equally be exploited by those with less altruistic motives.

There are also technical solutions that could discourage conspiracy. Bode and Vraga (2015) noted that even when exposed to factually incorrect information, the presence of correcting information in a "related stories" section resulted in a decrease in factually incorrect user beliefs. These "related stories" were manipulated artificially on Facebook in their study, but an appropriate algorithm could reproduce the effect. One concern was that implementation may in fact expose users to incorrect information due to a relationship with an otherwise correct article. Another is that their "correction" was only successful with respect to genetically modified organism beliefs and not with respect to anti-vaccination beliefs (Bode & Vraga, 2015).

Bricker's 2013 study on Climategate offers five suggestions on how scientists and environmentalists ought to respond to climate skeptics. The first is to use lay terminology to better interact with the public and avoid charges of elitism. The second is to better elucidate issues of scientific uncertainty and climatic unpredictability by focusing on the known elements, including known minimum risk (Bricker, 2013, p. 234). The third is to ensure peer review processes are "transparent, accountable, and welcoming of healthy skepticism" (Bricker, 2013, p. 234). Scientists must also become debaters and public speakers, by developing rhetorical skills. Finally, scientists must be prepared to counter criticism actively rather than letting their research offer its own defense (Bricker, 2013, p. 235).

To effectively engage in debate, those wishing to challenge conspiracy ought to understand conventional strategies used to bolster the defense of conspiracy theories. Kata (2012) offers 4 tactics and 14 overused themes of the anti-vaccination community along with counter-evidence, which offers a strong background for those attempting to engage directly with the anti-vaccination community. One element of note include "skewing the science," in which antivaccination members ignore evidence against their cause, and ignore problems with evidence in support of their cause (Kata, 2012, pp. 3781–3782). Another element worth mentioning are underhanded tactics, such as typosquatting, which refers to buying up common typos of the URLs of their opponents and redirecting it to their own page (Kata, 2012, p. 3782).

[...]

Conclusions

Despite the vast array of information we can access online, it is not a panacea for suspicious thinking or conspiracy theories. Some aspects that fuel conspiracy theories such as social exclusion are factors both online and off. Social media networks and search engines offer personalization algorithms which can increase polarization, and, based on research, seem to result in echo chambers of like-minded users. The accessibility of conflicting views does not guarantee we will choose to access them, or let them impact us.

However, there is no fundamental difference between how social media spreads scientific theories and conspiracy theories. The key differences were in how users reacted to posts. Conspiracy-polarized users were less likely to interact with contradictory posts, and more likely to be negative in their reactions. These negative reactions may reinforce feelings of social exclusion and further drive polarization. Echo bubbles of similar opinions form online, even among those who are not conspiracy theorists. We should expect conspiracy theorists to have built their own echo bubbles, which reinforce their beliefs.

Even though there may seem to be a moral imperative to intervene against the spread of conspiracy theories, active interventions are likely to violate the freedom of speech of conspiracy theorists. A better approach is to actively engage with and debate conspiracy theorists, presenting them with conflicting evidence and fostering a greater sense of social belonging. We should also aim to better understand the underlying beliefs and assumptions that guide users towards conspiracy theories in the first place.

Beyond active debate, there are also several policy changes that could influence the spread of conspiracy. Politically, free speech should be upheld as a universal human right, and impartial investigative procedures ought to be followed for major events. Greater information literacy among the general public will also assist with disrupting the future spread of conspiracy theories. Online developers should also consider the impact their algorithms may have on encouraging the formation of echo chambers or filter bubbles among users. Scientists must prepare to engage with people of all skill levels and to identify the root causes of hesitancy or doubt for certain key issues, such as vaccination.

References

Aupers, S. (2012). 'Trust no one': Modernization, paranoia and conspiracy culture. European Journal of Communication, 27(1), 22–34. doi:10.1177/0267323111433566

Bakshy, E., Messing, S., & Adamic, L. (2015). Exposure to ideologically diverse news and opinion on Facebook. Science. doi:10.1126/science.aaa1160

Bessi, A., Coletto, M., Davidescu, G. A., Scala, A., Caldarelli, G., & Quattrociocchi, W. (2015). Science vs conspiracy: Collective narratives in the age of misinformation. PLOS ONE, 10(2), e0118093. doi: 10.1371/journal.pone.0118093

Bessi, A., Zollo, F., Del Vicario, M., Puliga, M., Scala, A., Caldarelli, G., . . . Quattrociocchi, W. (2016). Users polarization on Facebook and YouTube. PLOS ONE, 11(8), 1–24. doi:10.1371/journal.pone.0159641

Bode, L., & Vraga, E. K. (2015). In related news, that was wrong: The correction of misinformation through related stories functionality in social media. Journal of Communication, 65(4), 619–638. doi:10.1111/jcom.12166

Bricker, B. J. (2013). Climategate: A case study in the intersection of facticity and conspiracy theory. Communication Studies, 64(2), 218– 239. doi:10.1080/10510974.20 12.749294

deHaven-Smith, L., & Witt, M. T. (2013). Conspiracy theory reconsidered: Responding to mass suspicions of political criminality in high office. Administration & Society, 45(3), 267–295. doi:10.1177/0095399712459727

Del Vicario, M., Bessi, A., Zollo, F., Petroni, F., Scala, A., Caldarelli, G., . . . Quattrociocchi, W. (2016). The spreading of misinformation online. Proceedings of the National Academy of Sciences of the United States of America, 113(3), 554–559. doi:10.1073/pnas.1517441113

Einstein, K. L., & Glick, D. M. (2015). Do I think BLS data are BS? The consequences of conspiracy theories. Political Behavior, 37(3), 679–701. doi:10.1007/s11109-014- 9287-z

Flaxman, S., Goel, S., & Rao, J. M. (2016). Filter bubbles, echo chambers, and online news consumption. Public Opinion Quarterly, 80, 298–320. doi:10.1093/poq/nfw006

Harambam, J., & Aupers, S. (2015). Contesting epistemic authority: Conspiracy theories on the boundaries of science. Public Understanding of Science, 24(4), 466–480. doi:10.1177/0963662514559891

Himelboim, I., McCreery, S., & Smith, M. (2013). Birds of a feather tweet together: Integrating network and content analyses to examine crossideology exposure on twitter. Journal of Computer-Mediated Communication, 18(2), 40–60. doi:10.1111/jcc4.12001

Jacobson, S., Myung, E., & Johnson, S. L. (2016). Open media or echo chamber: The use of links in audience discussions on the Facebook pages of partisan news organizations. Information, Communication & Society, 19(7), 875–891. doi:10.1080/136911 8X.2015.106446 1

Jong, W., & Dückers, M. L. A. (2016). Selfcorrecting mechanisms and echoeffects in social media: An analysis of the "gunman in the newsroom" crisis. Computers in Human Behavior, 59, 334–341. doi:10.1016/j.chb.2016.02.032

Kata, A. (2012). Anti-vaccine activists, web 2.0, and the postmodern paradigm– An overview of tactics and tropes used online by the anti-vaccination movement. Vaccine, 30(25), 3778–3789. doi: 10.1016/j.vaccine.2011.11.112

Martin, B. (2015). Censorship and free speech in scientific controversies. Science and Public Policy, 42(3), 377–386. doi:10.1093/scipol/scu061

Menchaca, F. (2012). The future is in doubt: Librarians, publishers, and networked learning in the 21st century. Journal of Library Administration, 52(5), 396–410. doi:10. 1080/01930826.2012.700804

Messing, S., & Westwood, S. J. (2014). Selective exposure in the age of social media: Endorsements trump partisan source affiliation when selecting news online. Communication Research, 41(8), 1042–1063. doi:10.1177/0093650212466406

Mocanu, D., Rossi, L., Zhang, Q., Karsai, M., & Quattrociocchi, W. (2015). Collective attention in the age of (mis)information. Computers in Human Behavior, 51, Part B, 1198– 1204. doi:10.1016/j.chb.2015.01.024

Nyhan, B. (2014). The myth of the ideological echo chamber. New York Times, 164(56666), 3–3. Retrieved from http://search.ebscohost.com/login.as px?direct=true&db=aph&AN=990426 77&site=ehost-live

Sunstein, C. R., & Vermeule, A. (2009). Conspiracy theories: Causes and cures. Journal of Political Philosophy, 17(2), 202–227. doi:10.1111/j.1467- 9760.2008.00325.x

Swami, V., Voracek, M., Stieger, S., Tran, U. S., & Furnham, A. (2014). Analytic thinking reduces belief in conspiracy theories. Cognition, 133(3), 572–585. doi:http://dx.doi.org/10.1016/j.cogniti on.2014.08.006

Tufekci, Z. (2015). Facebook said its algorithms do help form echo chambers, and the tech press missed it. NPQ: New Perspectives Quarterly, 32(3), 9–12. doi:10.1111/npqu.11519

Zollo, F., Novak, P. K., Del Vicario, M., Bessi, A., Mozetič, I., Scala, A., . . . Quattrociocchi, W. (2015). Emotional dynamics in the age of misinformation. PLOS ONE, 10(9), 1–22. doi:10.1371/journal.pone.0138740

> *"Students whose teachers believe they are stupid end up acting stupid— what happens when the filters decide we're dumb, or smart, or athletic, or right wing, or left wing?"*

Beware the Dark Side of Internet Personalization

Cory Doctorow

In the following viewpoint, Cory Doctorow uses Eli Pariser's hot-button and influential book The Filter Bubble: What the Internet Is Hiding from You *as a vehicle to express his own views on filters. One of Pariser's points the author agrees with is the editorial nature of filtering algorithms. While we think of the rankings as objective, there is actually an editorial element involved, just as a human editor would provide. The author takes issue with Pariser's forecasts for the future, but overall Doctorow believes that Pariser's book provides a valuable foundation for discussions about the future of content management. Doctorow is a copyright law activist, journalist, and coeditor of the blog Boing Boing.*

As you read, consider the following questions:

1. To what does Pariser compare having to tune out excessive messages, according to the author?
2. In what way does the author feel that Pariser's future projection is too static?
3. How does the author use the concept of a book review to develop and express his own views?

MoveOn co-founder Eli Pariser's new book *The Filter Bubble: What the Internet Is Hiding from You* is a thoughtful, often alarming look at the dark side of Internet personalization. Pariser is concerned that invisible "smart" customization of your Internet experience can make you parochial, exploiting your cognitive blind-spots to make you overestimate the importance or prevalence of certain ideas, products and philosophies and underestimate others. In Pariser's view, invisible, unaccountable, commercially driven customization turns into a media-bias-of-one, an information system that distorts your perception of reality. Pariser doesn't believe that this is malicious or intentional, but he worries that companies with good motives ("let's hide stuff you always ignore; let's show you search results similar to the kinds you've preferred in the past") and bad ("let's spy on your purchasing patterns to figure out how to trick you into buying stuff that you don't want") are inadvertently, invisibly and powerfully changing the discourse.

Pariser marshalls some good examples and arguments in favor of this proposition. Students whose teachers believe they are stupid end up acting stupid—what happens when the filters decide we're dumb, or smart, or athletic, or right wing, or left wing? He cites China and reiterates the good arguments we've heard from the likes of Rebecca McKinnon: that the Chinese politburo gets more political control over the way it shapes which messages and arguments you see (through paid astroturfers) than by mere censorship of the Internet. Pariser cites research from cognitive scientists and behavioral economists on how framing and presentation can radically alter our perception of events. Finally, he convincingly describes how a world of messages that you have to consciously tune out is different from one in which the tuning out is done automatically—for example, if you attend a town hall meeting in which time is taken up with discussion of issues that you don't care about, you still end up learning what your neighbors care about. This creates a shared frame of reference that strengthens your community.

Pariser also points out—correctly, in my view—that filtering algorithms are editorial in nature. When Google's programmers tweak and modify their ranking algorithm to produce a result that "feels" better (or that users click on more), they're making an editorial decision about what sort of response they want their search results to evince. Putting more-clicked things higher up is an editorial decision: "I want to provide you with the sort of information whose utility is immediately obvious." And while this is, intuitively, a useful way to present stuff, there's plenty of rewarding material whose utility can't be immediately divined or described (I thought of Jonah Lehrer's *How We Decide*, which describes an experiment in which subjects who were asked to explain why they liked certain pictures made worse choices than ones who weren't asked to explain their preferences). When we speak of Google's results as being driven by "relevance," we act as though there was a platonic, measurable, independent idea of "relevance" that was separate from judgment, bias, and editorializing. Some relevance can't be divined a priori—how relevant is an open window to Fleming's Petri dish?

There were places where I argued with Pariser's analysis, however. On the one hand, Pariser's speculation about the future seems overly speculative: "What if augmented reality as presently practiced by artists and futurists becomes commonplace?" On the other hand, Pariser's futures are too static: He presumes a world in which filtering tools become increasingly sophisticated, but anti-filtering tools (ad-blockers, filter-comparison tools, etc) remain at present-day levels. The first wave of personalization in the Web was all about changing how your browser displayed the information it received; the trend to modular, fluid site-design built around XML, CSS, DHTML, AJAX, etc, makes it even more possible to block, rearrange, and manage the way information is presented to you. That is, even as site designers are becoming increasingly sophisticated in the way they present their offerings to you, you are getting more and more power to break that presentation, to recombine it and filter it yourself. Filters that you create and maintain are probably subject to some of the dangers that Pariser fears, but they're also a powerful check against the alarming manipulation he's most anxious about. Pariser gives short shrift to this, dismissing the fact that the net makes it theoretically easier than ever to see what the unfiltered (or differently filtered) world looks like with hand-waving: the filters will make it so we don't even want to go outside of them.

I don't believe that anti-filters or personal filters will automatically act as a check against manipulative customization, but I believe that they have this *potential. The Filter Bubble* is mostly a story about potential—the potential of filtering technology to grow unchecked. And against that, I think it's worth discussing (and caring about, and working for) the potential of a technological response to that chilling future.

> *"In order to be informed citizens,
> students need to learn how to seek
> out, access, and analyze different
> types of information using media."*

Media Education Is a Tenet of Democratic Education

Jeremy Stoddard

In the following excerpted viewpoint, Jeremy Stoddard argues that strong media education is necessary in the digital age. Even though the Internet is flooded with information, the fact that most content comes from a relatively small number of "elite" sources rather than discourse by "the people," leads the author to believe that digital media has failed to make society more democratic. In addition, Stoddard contends, the rise of social media has created a deeper partisan divide among citizens. He proposes that we invest in media education in order to foster strong global citizenship. Stoddard is a professor of education, chair of the department of curriculum and instruction, associated faculty with the film and media studies program, and director of the interdisciplinary educational studies program at the College of William and Mary.

"The Need for MediaEducation in Democratic Education," by Jeremy Stoddard. Originally published in *Democracy & Education* vol 22, issue 1, 2014.

As you read, consider the following questions:

1. What aspects of a democratic society are improved by access to the internet?
2. What three aspects of media education does the author suggest are essential for democratic education for global citizenship?
3. How can simulations help students learn to act as global citizens, according to the author?

Is Society More Democratic in the 21st Century?

Given the increased access to information and abilities to communicate, the first issue to examine is whether or not the digital media and networks of the 21st century have led to a more democratic society. There is evidence that they have not. Hindman (2008) argues that despite the potential for broadened political discourse and the ability of marginalized groups to have a greater voice, the reality is that the vast amount of media traffic is still controlled by the political and media elite. This is not to say that marginalized voices are not present over the myriad of websites, blogs, Twitter feeds, and other social media sources and news streams, but the number of visitors to these sites represents a very small proportion of web users. The bulk of Internet users instead are visiting news sources controlled by, and thus accessing the information provided by, the global elite (Hindman, 2008).

There have also been, of course, radical changes in the digital age in the way politicians and individual citizens can mobilize support, transmit information, raise funds, and organize, but this is more limited than is commonly perceived (Loader & Mercea, 2012). This transformation has not necessarily given the public a larger voice or lessened the impact of corporate messages, as websites and media being used to voice populist political messages are getting very little attention.

The impact of media on politics, and in particular on the ability of political and economic elites to control political messages, has only grown since the 2009 *Citizens United U.S. Supreme Court* ruling that allows unlimited and virtually anonymous money to be given to super PAC organizations. The impact of these super PACs is up for debate, as many of the largest organizations on the conservative end of the political spectrum did not get much return on their donors' investments during the 2012 presidential election (Tumulty, 2012). However, that election as well as recent Senate, House, and even state-level elections have been the most expensive in history by wide margins (Confessore & Bidgood, 2012). Therefore, the need for a media-savvy society is more important to our democracy than ever. This means that citizens need to both understand the nature and power of political messages in media and be able to take advantage of new media and participatory culture in order to take action.

Media, Politics, and Society

A secondary issue, evident in the United States in particular, is the way that new media have served as a catalyst for the growing partisan divide in the citizenry. As a result of being able to control which news sources and media they access, citizens are no longer being exposed to the same type of broad-spectrum coverage that a trip to the newsstand would provide (Sunstein, 2007). In this way, the advent of new media may be contributing to a less democratic society, especially when the narrowing political perspectives are combined with lessening social and civic engagement among people from different economic classes or with different political, social, and religious views (Bishop, 2008; Putnam & Campbell, 2010).

Not only are citizens more likely to engage solely with views that already reflect their own, they are also likely to live in communities that also reflect these views (Bishop, 2008). According to Bishop, more people today are living near others who share similar backgrounds and views on politics, religion, and social issues as a result of racial desegregation and White flight, the development of gated and elite neighborhoods, and political gerrymandering.

The effects of this political, social, and class segregation mean that people are not being exposed to different political or social views and are not being engaged in discussions with people with divergent backgrounds. Elites' control of the information and perspectives that an individual will physically and virtually encounter during the day may in part foster the type of extreme political partisanship illustrated in the past five years in state elections and ballot initiatives, in Congress, and in the last two presidential elections (Sunstein, 2009). This is what Pariser (2011) refers to as the filter bubble—in essence, a system of algorithms built into search engines and social media that hone each individual's news feeds to unique preferences and thus control the news encountered.

Of course, this overview of American society does not fully explain the nature of youth civic engagement. Numerous studies have illustrated the nature and ability of young people to avoid the partisan trappings of older generations and find ways to engage— now using new media to communicate with others as close as next door or as far as all the way on the other side of the globe. In particular, youth are using the web and social media to form or join grassroots organizations and focus on local issues or issues related to identity politics in particular (Banaji, Buckingham, van Zoonen, & Hirzalla, 2009).

Similarly, work conducted by organizations such as the Center for Information & Research on Civic Learning & Engagement (CIRCLE) and the MacArthur Foundation's Research Network on Youth and Participatory Politics has identified the numerous ways in which young people engage civically and participate in politics online or using new media (e.g., Bennett, 2008; Cohen & Kahne, 2012). These studies show that young people are engaged in civic behaviors via social media, such as forwarding or otherwise sharing political cartoons or other messages from political organizations, posting to a discussion forum of a political organization or a news site, or joining a political group online. However, they are not as confident in judging the trustworthiness of sources or in recognizing political messages in less explicit media forms. Unfortunately, the development of skills and knowledge that take advantage of new media to engage in citizenship activities is extremely limited in the current standardized academic context in education (e.g., Au, 2007; Levine, Lopez, & Marcelo, 2008). These skills could include the development of the types of critical literacy deemed lacking or the ability to craft political messages using new media to create a campaign to advocate for a local issue.

[…]

What Does Education for Citizenship Look Like?

As I identified in the beginning of this essay, one of the major challenges in examining the relationship between citizenship and digital democracy is forming a consensus as to what it means to be a democratic citizen. Generally, there is an attempt to define *citizenship* through a framework of knowledge, skills, and dispositions (e.g., Gould, 2011). Knowledge can include understanding the structure of governments and international treaties or the history of human rights. Skills may include the ability to analyze and weigh evidence, answer complex problems, or communicate persuasively. Dispositions, often the most controversial, may to some mean the desire to vote, volunteer, or reflect good moral character. Others may envision the dispositions of a citizen to include goals of social justice and the role of citizens to actively work for equality in their communities or even act in civil disobedience to laws or actions they find unjust.

In order to be an effective citizen today, one must not limit citizenship to that of the nation-state. Given the nature of the global economy and ease in covering great distance using new media and networks, people in the current generation must be engaged as global citizens and prepared to consider a more diverse range of perspectives and issues than those of their parents and grandparents. The notion of global citizen reflects not just the role of the individual in the world but also the changing nature of the nation-state as populations become more global. According to

Banks (2008), the dispositions of global citizens in multicultural societies include a sense of cosmopolitanism where individuals

> view themselves as citizens of the world who will make decisions and take actions in the global interests that will benefit humankind. . . . Cosmopolitans identify with peoples from diverse cultures throughout the world . . . [and] are ready to broaden the definition of public, extend their loyalty beyond ethnic and national boundaries, and engage with difference far and near. (p. 134)

Banks does not argue that citizens should lack an allegiance to a national identity or a role as a national citizen but that they should be able to engage with others from around the world, make efforts to understand global perspectives, and consider the global consequences of decisions in addition to the personal, local, and national consequences. Similarly, Thornton (2005) states "although educating for internationalism often seeks to eliminate exploitation, militarism, and national vainglory it is nonetheless reconcilable with a reasoned loyalty to a nation-state" (p. 82). Therefore, one of the goals in developing global citizens is that they understand the value in attempting to consider issues from global perspectives as well as national viewpoints.

When we attempt to identify the specific characteristics, including the knowledge, skills, and dispositions, of this kind of citizen, they would likely include: (a) the ability to examine problems and issues from multiple perspectives, find and weigh evidence, and deliberate and come to reasoned conclusions (Hess, 2009; Parker, 2003); (b) the ability to take actions not only as a participatory citizen but one who is justice oriented to work for the common good globally and locally (Westheimer & Kahne, 2004); and (c) the knowledge of the workings of government and power from the local to the global and an understanding that a citizen's role is to continually seek out knowledge and recognize the constructed and often contested nature of knowledge (Gould, 2011). All of these characteristics require that citizens understand the nature of media and information they engage with, the ability to use media to communicate and persuade others, and the most effective ways to organize and take action.

Media Education as Part of Global Democratic Citizenship Education

What would the integration of media education into democratic education look like in the schools, curriculum, and teacher education? How can media help to foster aspects of citizenship and understandings needed for a global society? Further, what research needs to be done to fully understand how best to prepare active global citizens for our new-media world? There are three interrelated aspects of media education that I pose as being central to strengthening democratic education for global citizenship: the need for a fundamental understanding of the nature of media, the use of simulations of democratic processes and practices, and the explicit development of media education skills for strong democratic citizenship. In the end, it may be that we need to rethink the nature of our citizenship education programs and the vision for global democratic citizens who can best meet the challenges of the 21st century—a model of citizenship education centered around participatory and strong democracy in a mediated society.

Understanding Media

I have made the case here that separate courses in technology and media literacy or the incorporation of media literacy into the English or literature curriculum are not meeting the needs of citizenship education. This does not mean that the underlying frameworks from these curricula need to go out with the proverbial bathwater. The most important lesson that can be drawn from earlier renditions from media education, or what Hoechsmann and Poyntz (2012) refer to as Media Literacy 1.0, is the need to help teachers and students to form an understanding of the nature of media.

Put differently, in order to develop a more critical viewpoint on information and technologies, one must first have a basic epistemological view of media representations as constructed and their delivery technologies as designed for particular purposes and not as neutral tools. This includes all forms of mediated information: visual media such as films, video, and video games; various textual sources of media including socially constructed wikis, blogs, and discussion forums; data-driven sites that present data in visual or even interactive ways; and social media that contain all of these media forms. All of these media forms represent data using symbol systems that reflect particular histories and social and cultural viewpoints and hold power. Understanding of the nature of media prepares teachers and students to be able to recognize that the media they engage with reflect particular viewpoints constructed within a particular context. This means that the analysis of media needs to go beyond the diegesis, or "content" of the media, to also examine the context of its production and dissemination and perspectives of its authors. Further, concepts from political communications that explain how media messages are used to prime and frame messages—and the thinking and discussions they promote—may be helpful in understanding the nature of media communication.

The goal of understanding the nature of media is twofold. First, critical scholars views that media representations hold power and most often work to recreate social and political hierarchies is still relevant today, as Hindman's (2008) work illustrates. Therefore, it is important to develop student citizens who critically analyze the information they consume and reflect upon how the technologies they use shape how they may be accessing information and how they view the world. This understanding is particularly necessary for global citizenship as the issues of power are exacerbated by the barriers between countries and peoples identified as "developed" versus "developing" and the role of media in countries where it is used to control populations or used to de ne the relations between nations. However, as Ellsworth (1989) eloquently noted, critical pedagogy can be highly impractical.

Therefore, there is a second pragmatic goal for understanding the nature of media representations. In order to use media effectively toward democratic goals, students must understand how media are constructed to evoke emotion, persuade an audience, and connect with others. Most important, a focus on media understanding versus the use of technologies as tools is advantageous. Once students have a fundamental understanding of the nature of media, they can continue to apply that understanding even as media forms converge and evolve or the delivery technologies change.

There are many activities that can be done to help students build these reflexive habits: reverse-storyboarding political advertisements, comparing and contrasting global newspaper headlines on political issues or films from different periods that represent the same event or topic, producing a video or video game and reflecting on all of the decisions made to construct it. There are also basic critical media literacy skills that come from understanding media production and heuristic lessons that may be helpful to form this understanding, such as how camera angles are used to evoke particular emotions and identities, how racial and gender stereotypes have developed over time, or how search engines function to produce results. The understanding of the nature of media and the power of media in global politics provides a foundation to develop further comprehension of democratic processes and practices and the explicit skills necessary to effectively engage as a global citizen.

Simulating Democratic Processes and Practices

The one section of *The Civic Mission of Schools* (Gould, 2011) report that includes a specific mention of the use of media is the "proven practice" they identify as "simulations of democratic processes" (p. 34). In the report, simulations are presented as motivating and as models in which students can practice skills and apply their civic knowledge. Although simulations in different forms have been used in social studies classes for decades, the number of video games and digital simulations related to civic education has expanded greatly over the past decade. Any motivation that these games provide may be the result of the authenticity of the experience and the ability of students to engage in realistic issues or problems with fellow students more than that students are engaged in a game or mediated simulation. After all, the games created for educational use generally do not rival the production quality or game design of their commercial counterparts.

The real value, alluded to in *The Civic Mission of Schools* (2011) report but not fully explored, is the ability to engage students in developing the epistemologies of practice of disciplines or positions related to active citizenship. Shaffer (2006), in his studies of the use of games for learning, focuses on how games can be used as models for learning to engage students in professional practices of different disciplines. For example, how better to learn how to use evidence to take a position and attempt to persuade others of your position's warrant than to work from the role of a member of Congress or community activist? If you want to learn about global political, social, or environmental issues impacting a particular part of the world, why not engage in those situations from the role of an aid worker, journalist, local activist, or diplomat? Being placed in these roles and having to engage in different situations can help students learn about contemporary issues, learn about the relationships between different countries or groups of people around the globe, and learn the tools, practices, and goals of different relevant perspectives.

Other games and simulations have been developed to simulate civic action on a more local level. Two games developed by Squire and his colleagues, *Greenbush* and *Dow Day*, attempt to leverage the gaming model to local history and civic engagement. *Greenbush* is an augmented reality game developed in large part by students that engages middle school students in learning about their local community as they explore the neighborhood physically and virtually using mobile devices. As they explore the Madison, Wisconsin, Greenbush neighborhood, they are able to access relevant images, documents, and information about the history of and events that occurred in their community. The students who designed this game and conducted the historical inquiry on the neighborhood worked to establish a Greenbush Day in Madison to celebrate the historical significance of the neighborhood (csumc. wisc.edu/cmct/greenbush/index.htm).

The same augmented reality game development group (ARIS) developed another place-based game that helped students explore the historic Dow Chemical lab bombing on the University of Wisconsin-Madison campus during the Vietnam War (http:// arisgames.org/featured/dow-day/). These situational, local, and augmented reality games are poignant for students learning how to engage locally and may be particularly useful for encouraging younger students to take a more active civic action stance. Simulations can be a place where developing citizens learn and practice civic action and develop civic knowledge. Of course, as Raphael, Bachen, Lynn, Baldwin-Philippi, and McKee (2010) remind, it is still important to ask students to reflect on how the game was designed to engage them from a particular perspective and to look at the context of who made the game and its goals— reinforcing the importance of always thinking about the nature of media, how it is constructed, and to what end.

Developing the Skills of Global Citizens

Simulations can help students to learn and practice skills that are important to taking effective action as a global citizen. It is important to follow playing games or participating in simulations with an examination of what was learned and how the skills and knowledge gained might be used outside of the simulated world. These include how to access, analyze, and use evidence to persuade others; how to discuss and deliberate controversial public issues; and how to participate as a citizen, from voting to taking action through civil disobedience or collective action (Gould, 2011; Hess, 2009; Parker, 2003). Many of these skills emerge from the types of literacy work identified in the Common Core Standards included above. However, these standards more accurately reflect the types of disciplinary literacy associated with literary or historical work and not those of a citizen. What, then, are important areas from media education that align with the goals of global citizenship? Once students gain a fundamental understanding of the nature of media and how media are used within the different disciplines or epistemologies of practice associated with politics or civic action, they can apply these lessons using different media forms and techniques.

In order to be informed citizens, students need to learn how to seek out, access, and analyze different types of information using media. They need to know how to use databases, computational media for using and analyzing data, and media tools to help to organize and capture information. They also need to engage in communication and deliberation with others, ideally around the globe. Therefore, they need to understand how to use communications technologies as well as how to apply their understanding of media and their desire to understand issues from different perspectives. In addition to media that allow for direct communication with others using text, video, or audio, fundamental skills of clear communication through writing or visual means are also vital. This means formal skills in being able to use different forms of evidence to persuade others are as relevant today as they were when the primary delivery technology was written correspondence.

Finally, specific techniques gleaned from understanding contemporary practices of political and civic action can be honed. These include using techniques in social media to create networks of like-minded citizens as well as using specific media forms such as editorials, blogs, tweets, and media-generated ash mobs to reach and persuade people. They can also study election or issue-based campaigns to identify strategies used. For example, the architects of the recent campaign in the state of Minnesota against a traditional marriage amendment used their understanding of the people of the state to persuade them to vote down the amendment. They were successful because they were able to appeal to the religious, civic, and social beliefs of the majority of the population through local television and radio advertisements and interviews and collaborate with sympathetic groups as a result of get-out-the-vote networking and ground campaigns. Examining cases of civic action in practice and identifying and practicing the skills necessary to be effective in these cases are important steps to becoming a global citizen—as important as having a cosmopolitan view of the world or the desire to help to take action in a local community or on an international issue.

Making Media Education Core to Democratic Education

The three applications of media education in democratic education are not intended to be fully inclusive of how these two areas are intertwined or complementary. Instead, they are intended to start a conversation about how media education may be more effectively integrated into disciplines such as democratic education—where there is an added value to applying disciplinary and specific concepts of media and actions with media.

I would be wrong to not point out the obvious—that all of the activities above would be worthless without a well-trained teacher or facilitator to lead them. Media education and citizenship education are complex content areas that require deep thinking and reflection. Teachers need to provide the kind of open classroom climate, willingness to engage students in controversial issues, and confidence to let students explore their own political and civic identities in which these types of strategies might work (McAvoy & Hess, 2013). In order to make this possible, teacher education programs must incorporate democratic pedagogy and media education more explicitly in their programs.

In addition to teachers, school leaders need to be willing to revisit media policies to allow such activities to be supported, and state policymakers need to take the political and moral imperative to construct state standards and curricula that emphasize a model of active global citizenship, and they all need trust that students will be encouraged to find their own place on the political spectrum and that the knowledge, skills, and dispositions described above are applicable regardless of political identity.

Finally, researchers must continue to explore the implications for media education within democratic education. They also must examine how media can be integrated into different educational contexts. Many of the studies cited in this paper are from research done outside of the typical school schedule and setting. One question is, how can simulations, critical media literacy, and democratic pedagogies reach students in the poorest and least well-equipped schools? After all, these are the students who most need access to high-quality curriculum and instruction. They are also exactly the young citizens we want to equip to take civic action locally and globally.

References

Au, W. (2007). High-stakes testing and curricular control: A qualitative metasynthesis. *Educational Researcher, 36*(5), 258–267.

Banaji, S., Buckingham, D., Van Zoonen, L., & Hirzalla, F. (2009). *Synthesis of Civic Web results and policy outcomes.* London, U.K.: Institute of Education, University of London.

Banks, J. A. (2008). Diversity, group identity, and citizenship education in a global age. *Educational Researcher, 37*(3), 129–139.

Bennett, W. L. (2008). Changing citizenship in the digital age. In W. L. Bennett (Ed.), Civic life online: Learning how digital media can engage youth (pp. 1 –24). Cambridge, MA: The MIT Press.

Bishop, B. (2008). *The big sort: Why the clustering of like-minded American is tearing us apart.* New York, NY: Houghton Mifflin.

Buckingham, D. (2000). *The making of citizens.* London, U.K.: Routledge. Buckingham, D. (2009). In defence of media studies. *The Guardian.* Retrieved from

http://www.guardian.co.uk/commentisgree/2009/aug/22/media-studies

Cohen, C., & Kahne, J. (2012). *Participatory politics: New media and youth political action.* Civic Education Research Group. Retrieved from http://civicsurvey.org/ YPP_Survey_Report_FULL.pdf

Common Core State Standards Initiative. (2010). *Common core state standards for English language arts & literacy in history/social studies, science, and technical subjects.* Retrieved from http://www.corestandards.org/the-standards/download-the-standards

Confessore, N. & Bidgood, J. (2012, November 7). Little to show for cash flood by big donors. *The New York Times.* Retrieved from http://www.nytimes.com/2012/11/08/ us/ politics/little-to-show-for-cash-flood-by-big-donors. html?hp&pagewanted=print &_r=0

Cuban, L. (1986). *Teachers and machines: The classroom use of technology since 1920*. New York, NY: Teachers College Press.

Cuban, L. (2001). *Oversold and underused: Computers in the classroom*. Cambridge, MA: Harvard University Press.

Ellsworth, E. (1989). Why doesn't this feel empowering? Working through the repressive myths of critical pedagogy. *Harvard Educational Review, 59*(3), 297–325.

DeWitt, S. W. (2007). Dividing the digital divide: Instructional use of computers in social studies. *Theory & Research in Social Education, 35*(2), 277–304.

Gee, J. P. (2013). *The anti-education era: Creating smarter students through digital learning*. New York, NY: Palgrave Macmillan.

Gee, J. P. (2007). What video games have to teach us about learning and literacy (2nd ed.). New York, NY: Palgrave Macmillan.

Gould, J. (2011). *Guardian of democracy: The civic mission of schools*. Philadelphia, PA: Annenberg Public Policy Center of the University of Pennsylvania.

Hess, D. (2009). *Controversy in the classroom: The democratic power of discussion*. New York, NY: Routledge.

Hindman, M. (2008). *The myth of digital democracy*. Princeton, NJ: Princeton University Press.

Hoechsmann, M., & Poyntz, S. (2012). *Media literacies: A critical introduction*. London, U.K.: Wiley-Blackwell.

Jenkins, H. (2006). *Convergence culture: Where old and new media collide*. New York, NY: New York University Press.

Kellner, D. (2009). Toward a critical media/cultural studies. In R. Hammer & D. Kellner (Eds.), *Media/cultural studies: Critical approaches* (pp. 5–24). New York, NY: Peter Lang.

Kellner, D., & Share, J. (2007). Critical media literacy, democracy, and the reconstruction of education. In D. Macedo & S. R. Steinberg (Eds.), *Media literacy: A reader* (pp. 3–23). New York, NY: Peter Lang.

Ladson-Billings, G. (2005). Differing concepts of citizenship: Schools and communities as sites of civic development. In N. Noddings (Ed.), *Educating citizens for global awareness.* (pp. 69–80). New York, NY: Teachers College Press.

Levine, P., Lopez, M. H., & Marcelo, K. B. (2008). Getting narrower at the base: e American curriculum after NCLB. Medford, MA: CIRCLE (The Center for Information & Research on Civic Learning & Engagement). Retrieved from http:// www.civicyouth. org/PopUps/Narrowing_Curriculum.pdf

Loader, B., & Mercea, D. (Eds.). (2012). *Social media and democracy: Innovations in participatory politics*. New York, NY: Routledge.

Margolis, J. (2008). *Stuck in the shallow end: Education, race, and computing*. Cambridge, MA: The MIT Press.

McAvoy, P., & Hess, D. (2013). Classroom deliberation in an era of political polarization. *Curriculum Inquiry, 43*(1), 14–47.

National Council for the Social Studies. (2009). Media Literacy Position Statement. Retrieved from www.socialstudies.org/positions/medialiteracy

National Council for the Social Studies. (2010). *National curriculum standards for social studies: A framework for teaching, learning, and assessment.* Atlanta, GA: NCSS Publications.

National Council for the Social Studies. (2013). Technology Position Statement. Retrieved from www.socialstudies.org/positions/technology

Pariser, L. (2011). *The filter bubble: What the Internet is hiding from you.* London, U.K.: Penguin Press.

Parker, W. (2003). *Teaching democracy: Unity and diversity in public life.* New York, NY: Teachers College Press.

Postman, N. (1992). Technopoly: The surrender of culture to technology. New York, NY: Vintage Books.

Putnam, R. D., & Campbell, D. E. (2010). *American grace: How religion divides and unites us.* New York, NY: Simon & Schuster.

Raphael, C., Bachen, C., Lynn, K. M., Baldwin-Philippi, J., & McKee, K. A. (2010). Games for civic learning: A conceptual framework and agenda for research and design. *Games and Culture, 5*(2), 199–235.

Sha er, D. W. (2006). *How computer games help children learn.* New York, NY: Palgrave Macmillan.

Sunstein, C. (2007). *Republic.com 2.0.* Princeton, NJ: Princeton University Press.

Sunstein, C. (2009). *Going to extremes: How like minds unite and divide.* Oxford, U.K.: Oxford University Press.

Thornton, S. (2005). Incorporating internationalism into the social studies curriculum. In N. Noddings (Ed.), *Educating citizens for global awareness* (pp. 81–92). New York, NY: Teachers College Press.

Tumulty, K. (2012, November 1,). Karl Rove and his super PAC vow to press on. *The Washington Post.* Retrieved from http://articles.washingtonpost.com/2012-11-10/politics/35506918_1_american-crossroads-crossroads-gps-pacs

U.K. Department for Education. (2007). The national curriculum: Citizenship programmes of study for key stages 3–4. London, UK: Department for Education. Retrieved from http://www.education.gov.uk/schools/teachingandlearning/curriculum/secondary/b00199157/citizenship/ks4/programme

U.K. Department for Education. (2013). National curriculum in England: Citizenship programmes of study for key stages 3 and 4. London, UK: Department for Education. Retrieved from https://www.gov.uk/government/publications/ national-curriculum-in-england-citizenship-programmes-of-study

Washington State Social Studies Learning Standards. (2008). Retrieved from http://www.k12.wa.us/socialstudies

Westheimer, J., & Kahne, J. (2004). What kind of citizen? The politics of educating for democracy. *American educational research journal, 41*(2), 237–269.

> *"People who are offline are more likely to be socially isolated and have less diverse social relationships, thereby being exposed to less-diverse ideas and viewpoints."*

Online Filter Bubbles May Impact Our Votes

Dominic DiFranzo and Kristine Gloria-Garcia

In the following viewpoint, Dominic DiFranzo and Kristine Gloria-Garcia argue that social media played an important role in two of 2016's defining events. The authors point to studies that show that online filter bubbles and the spread of fake news have direct effects on the opinions we form and the actions we take. In the case of the 2016 presidential election, social media—including bot-generated tweets—played an important part in voters' opinions and actions. The authors conclude by questioning how technical improvements can be balanced with First Amendment rights to ensure a stable democracy. DiFranzo is a postdoctoral associate in the social media lab at Cornell University. Gloria-Garcia is a project manager for the Aspen Institute Communications and Society Program.

"Filter Bubbles and Fake News," by Dominic DiFranzo and Kristine Gloria-Garcia, ACM, Inc, April 2017. Reprinted by permission.

As you read, consider the following questions:

1. How did Mark Zuckerberg respond to allegations that Facebook influenced the 2016 election?
2. What percentage of millennials use Facebook to consume news stories?
3. What percentage of pro-Trump tweets came from automated bots, according to a study cited in the viewpoint?

T he E.U. referendum in the U.K. and the U.S. presidential election shocked journalists, pollsters, and citizens around the world. The outcomes—the U.K. voting to leave the EU and Donald Trump being elected President—raise the question of how traditional media and polls could have been so wrong in their predictions.[1] While plenty of fingers still point to outside interference, changing demographics, and economic concerns, one scapegoat— social media—has received extra-special attention. Some critics place the fault with Facebook, Google, and other social media platforms for allowing the spread of "fake news," pointing to, for example, the creation and facilitation of echo chambers, where users are no longer exposed to outside options and views.[2] *The New York Times* reported that following Trump's victory, executives at Facebook began to privately consider the role their company and platform had on the election.[1] However, Facebook CEO Mark Zuckerberg downplayed the company's role in the election, saying, "Voters make decisions based on their lived experience" and the theory that fake news shared on Facebook "influenced the election in any way, is a pretty crazy idea."[3]

So we ask, did social media play a role in these election upsets? In this article, we examine whether social media really did play a role, if fake news and filter bubbles had an effect, and if they did, what can be done about it in the future.

Social Media Effect

Social media trends (in terms of, say, numbers of posts, shares, and likes) on the day of the elections favored both Brexit and Trump,[4] which ran counter to the narrative of reputable polling and traditional media. Trump had more followers across social media platforms. He did, however, and continues to, push his messages through social media rather than traditional media channels, and had higher engagement rates compared to his opponent. One of the most shared posts on social media leading to the election was "Why I'm Voting For Donald Trump," a blog by a well-known conservative female blogger.[4] The trend was similar during the E.U. Referendum in the U.K. The official "Leave" campaign had more followers and engagement on social media platforms, as well as more success in spreading pro-leave hashtags and messages.[5]

Moreover, according to Pew Research, 61% of millennials use Facebook as their primary source for political news.[6] Such news has been shown to have a direct effect on political actions, attitudes, and outcomes. In 2012, a study reported in *Nature* described a randomized controlled trial of political mobilization messages delivered to 61 million Facebook users during the 2010 U.S. congressional elections. It found the messages directly influenced political self-expression, information seeking, and real-world voting behavior.[7] This is not surprising, as the dominant funding strategy of most social-media platforms follows the assumption that sponsored social-media posts, or advertisements, can change the buying behavior of their users.[8] In another example, the past decade has seen a rise in political movements (such as the Arab Spring and Black Lives Matter) that start on and are sustained through social-media platforms like Twitter and Facebook.

Hampton and Hargittai[9] offered evidence that the demographic most disconnected from social media and the web was also the most likely to be Trump supporters. Voters without a college degree supported Trump by a nine-percentage-point margin, whereas in past elections they were equally likely to support Democrats as Republicans. These gaps widen greatly when pollsters looked at white non-college-educated voters, who supported Trump by 39 percentage points in 2016, the largest margin of support from this demographic since 1980.[9] This group in particular—white noncollege-educated—were also most likely to not have access to the Internet, and of those who did were most likely to not use social media.[6]

Additionally, Pew Research reported that while millennials (people born 1977 to 1995) get their political news from social-media platforms, most Americans still rely on their local TV news stations and other traditional mass-media sources.[6] These are the same mass-media sources where Trump received significantly more attention and coverage compared to Hillary Clinton.[6] And while social-media-savvy millennials overwhelmingly supported Clinton, voter turnout from this demographic was lower than in both the 2008 and 2012 presidential elections. Further data analysis shows Clinton supporters were most likely to be engaged on social media platforms like Twitter and Reddit.[9]

Why then did a first-pass look at social data trends show more support for Trump than Clinton if social-media users seemed to show more support for Clinton? The answer is still being investigated, but one answer may be botnets. Two recent studies— one from researchers at the University of Southern California and the other from Oxford University, the University of Washington, and Corvinus University of Budapest—both showed AI-controlled bots were spreading pro-Trump content in overwhelming numbers. Kollanyi et al.[11] from Oxford University estimate that one-third of pro-Trump tweets came from automated bots, which they classified by how often these accounts tweeted, at what time of day, and their relation to other accounts. This created the illusion of more support for Trump on Twitter than there may have been naturally.[10,11] Kollanyi et al.[11] noted similar automated patterns on Twitter leading up to the EU referendum in the U.K. in which pro-Leave tweets greatly outnumbered pro-Stay tweets.

Filter Bubble

Another criticism of social media is that it constructs "filter bubbles," digital echo chambers where users see content and posts that agree only with their preexisting beliefs.[12] While there is an active dialogue taking place as to whether filter bubbles exist, here, we highlight work that explores whether it contributed to the 2016 election results.

In 2015, Facebook funded a study that showed that while Facebook's own newsfeed algorithm might favor posts that support a user's political beliefs, the related filter-bubble effect is due to the user's network and past engagement behavior (such as clicking only on certain news stories); that is, it is not the fault of the news-feed algorithm but the choices of users themselves. They also found this favoritism effect is small overall. The study showed users are only 6% less likely to see a post that conflicts with their political views when compared to an unfiltered newsfeed.[13]

Personal recommendation systems, or systems that learn and react to individual users, are claimed to be one cause of filter bubbles.[12] Other studies have shown that personalized recommendations can actually expose users to content they might not have found on their own[14] and that personalized recommendations are not used as extensively as once thought.[15] A 2011 national survey by Pew Research found Facebook use is actually correlated with knowing and interacting with a greater variety people from different backgrounds and demographics.[16] This correlation persists despite controlling for the demographic characteristics of Facebook users compared the U.S. population as a whole. In a sense, social media may actually be bursting filter bubbles. This same survey showed that people who are offline are more likely to be socially isolated and have less diverse social relationships, thereby being exposed to less-diverse ideas and viewpoints.[16]

While the studies are compelling, evidence of filter bubbles and their effect on users continues to grow. For example, several researchers have criticized the 2015 Facebook news-feed study mentioned earlier. Specifically, Zeynep Tufekci rebutted many of the findings and methodology of the study,[17] accusing it of underplaying its most important conclusion that the newsfeed algorithm decides placement of posts and this placement greatly influences what users click and read. Tufekci also highlighted that the sampling was not random and thus cannot be generalized across all Facebook users. Even if one takes the Facebook study at face value, it still shows the filter-bubble effect is real and the algorithm actively suppresses posts that conflict with a user's political viewpoint. Other recent studies (such as Del Vicario et al.[18] on the sharing of scientific and conspiracy stories on Facebook) found evidence of the formation of echo chambers that cause "confusion about causation, and thus encourage speculation, rumors, and mistrust."

Fake News

On the theme of "speculation, rumors, and mistrust," fake news is another issue that has plagued social media platforms during, as well as after, the U.S. elections. Fake news is a recent popular and purposefully ambiguous term for false news stories that are packaged and published as if they were genuine. The ambiguity of this term—an inherent property of what it tries to label— makes its use attractive across the political spectrum, where any information that conflicts with an ideology can be labeled "fake." The *Times* published an article[19] chronicling the spread of fake news on social media, saying one such fake story was shared at least 16,000 times on Twitter and more than 350,000 times on Facebook. According to BuzzFeed [20],[20] in the months before the U.S. elections, fake news stories on Facebook actually outperformed real news from mainstream news outlets. BuzzFeed[20] said these fake news stories overwhelmingly favored Trump. For example, a fake news story reported that Pope Francis endorsed Trump and was shared more than one million times on social media feeds. Pope Francis, an advocate for refugees, made no such endorsement. Not only were these fake news sources shared on social media platforms they were also shared by Trump himself, as well as by members of his campaign.[9]

Fake news stories have a real effect offline as well. A shooting took place in a Washington, D.C., pizzeria called Comet Ping Pong after fake news stories and conspiracy theories spread about it being part of a child trafficking ring.[21] Army Lt. Gen. Michael Flynn (Ret.), an early National Security Adviser under Trump, shared fake news stories related to this so-called "Pizza-gate" scandal more than 16 times, according to a Politico review of his Twitter posts.[22]

Although fake news may be a problem (though not uniquely to social media), its dissemination may not break out of the filter bubble at its point of origin. Several studies have shown the spread of fake news is similar to epidemics compared to real news stories and that such stories usually stay within the same communities[23]; that is, these stories tend to not reach or convince outsiders. Likewise, Mark Zuckerberg said in a Facebook post following the U.S. election, "Of all the content on Facebook, more than 99% of what people see is authentic. Only a very small amount is fake news and hoaxes. Overall, this makes it extremely unlikely hoaxes changed the outcome of this election in one direction or the other."[3] He did not provide any data or evidence to back this claim.

As the dust continues to settle from the election, research into the role of social media and digital media platforms as key influencers will continue. We acknowledge how unlikely it is analysts will ever reach a commonly accepted explanation for the election outcomes. However, it is imperative to acknowledge the need to study such potential cause and effects. We have thus laid out the potential research questions; we now turn to possible solutions.

Future Solutions

Even though fake news and filter bubbles are a problem that indeed affected the U.S. presidential election, social media platforms like Facebook and Google are exploring ways to reduce these influences on their platforms. Both Google and Facebook announced (November 2016) the banning of websites that publish fake news from their advertising networks, effectively killing the revenue stream of these sites.[24] Facebook has also created new tools to flag fake content and is partnering with third-party fact-checking organizations like Snopes and Politifact.[25] It is also developing better automatic fake-news-detection systems that will limit the spread of such content.

Researchers and software developers have been looking into tools to help break out of filter bubbles [26], including filtering algorithms and user interfaces that give users better control and allow more diversity. Other tools (such as browser plugin Ghostery and search engine DuckDuckGo) are being developed to help anonymize users' actions online, thus disabling personalized recommendations.

Bot and spam detection is another major area of research. Many social-media platforms already use a range of tools, from machine learning to social network analysis, to detect and stop bots. Independent groups and researchers have also developed tools to detect f; for example, researchers at Indiana University have developed BotOrNot (http://truthy.indiana.edu/botornot/), a service that allows users to check if a particular Twitter user is, in fact, a bot.

Difficult Questions

In addition to technical enhancements and design choices, what other avenues, even public policymaking, are available for combating these issues? This may be a particularly difficult question in the U.S. due to free-speech protections under the First Amendment of the U.S. Constitution. We already see legal and political tension as Twitter implements internal policies for flagging hate speech and closing specific accounts. Others have suggested a reinstatement of media- and civic-literacy initiatives to help users discern for themselves which news sources are indeed trustworthy.

These issues of fake news and filter bubbles are vague, nuanced, and pre-date social media, with no ready solution, but it is vital that researchers continue to explore and investigate them from diverse technical and social perspectives. Their skills, knowledge, and voices are needed more than ever to address them.

References

[1] Isaac, M. Facebook, in cross hairs after election, is said to question its influence. *The New York Times* (Nov. 12, 2016); https://www.nytimes.com/2016/11/14/technology/facebook-is-said-to-question-its-influence-in-election.html

[2] Isaac, M. and Ember, S. For election day influence, Twitter ruled social media. *The New York Times* (Nov. 8, 2016); http://www.nytimes.com/2016/11/09/technology/for-election-day-chatter-twitter-ruled-social-media.html

[3] Kokalitcheva, K. Mark Zuckerberg says fake news on Facebook affecting the election is a 'crazy idea.' *Fortune* (Nov. 11, 2016); http://fortune.com/2016/11/11/facebook-election-fake-news-mark-zuckerberg/?iid=sr-link1

[4] El-Bermawy, M.M. Your filter bubble is destroying democracy. *Wired* (Nov. 18, 2016); https://www.wired.com/2016/11/filter-bubble-destroying-democracy/

[5] Sigdyal, P. and Wells, N. Twitter users scream 'leave' in Brexit vote, but 'remain' gains ground. *CNBC* (June 23, 2016); http://www.cnbc.com/2016/06/23/twitter-users-scream-leave-in-brexit-vote-but-remain-gains-ground.html

[6] Mitchell, A., Gottfried, J., and Matsa, K.E. Facebook top source for political news among millennials. *Pew Research Center,* June 1, 2015; http://www.journalism.org/2015/06/01/facebook-top-source-for-political-news-among-millennials/

[7] Bond, R.M., Fariss, C.J., Jones, J.J., Kramer, A.D.I., Marlow, C., Se le, J.E., and Fowler, J.H. A 61-million-person experiment in social influence and political mobilization. *Nature 489,* 7415 (Sept. 2012), 295–298.

[8] Taylor, D.G., Lewin, J.E., and Strutton, D. Friends, fans, and followers: Do ads work on social networks? *Journal of Advertising Research 51,* 1 (2011), 258–275.

[9] Hampton, K. and Hargittai, E. Stop blaming Facebook for Trump's election win. *The Hill* (Nov. 23, 2016); http://thehill.com/blogs/pundits-blog/presidential-campaign/307438-stop-blaming-facebook-for-trumps-election-win

[10] Fields, J., Sengupta, S., White, J., Spetka, S. et al. *Botnet Campaign Detection on Twitter.* Master of science thesis in computer and information Sciences, Department of Computer Sciences, SUNY Polytechnic Institute, Utica, NY, 2016; https://dspace.sunyconnect.suny.edu/handle/1951/68351

[11] Kollanyi, B., Howard, P.N., and Woolley, S.C. Bots and automation over Twitter during the third U.S. presidential debate. *Political Bots* (Oct. 27, 2016); http://politicalbots.org/wp-content/uploads/2016/10/Data-Memo-Third-Presidential-Debate.pdf

[12] Pariser, E. *The Filter Bubble: How the New Personalized Web Is Changing What We Read and How We Think.* Penguin, New York, 2011.

[13] Bakshy, E., Messing, S., and Adamic, L. Exposure to ideologically diverse news and opinion on Facebook. *Science 348,* 6239 (2015), 1130–1132.

[14] Hosanagar, K., Fleder, D., Lee, D., and Buja, A. Will the global village fracture into tribes? Recommender systems and their effects on consumer fragmentation. *Management Science 60,* 4 (2013), 805–823.

[15] Weisberg, J. Bubble trouble: Is web personalization turning us into solipsistic twits. *Slate* (June 10, 2011); http://www.slate.com/articles/news_and_politics/the_big_idea/2011/06/bubble_trouble.html

[16] Hampton, K., Sessions Goulet, L., Rainie, L., and Purcell, K. Social networking sites and our lives. *Pew Research*, June 16, 2011; http://www.pewinternet.org/2011/06/16/social-networking-sites-and-our-lives/

[17] Tufekci, Z. How Facebook's algorithm suppresses content diversity (modestly) and how the newsfeed rules the clicks. *Medium* (May 7, 2015); https://medium.com/message/how-facebook-s-algorithm-suppresses-content-diversity-modestly-how-the-newsfeed-rules-the-clicks-b5f8a4bb7bab#.kw4xqeif0

[18] Del Vicario, M., Bessi, A., Zollo, F., Petroni, F., Scala, A., Caldarelli, G., Stanley, E., and Quattrociocchi, W. The spreading of misinformation online. *Proceedings of the National Academy of Sciences 113*, 3 (2016), 554–559.

[19] Maheshwari, S. How fake news goes viral: A case study. *The New York Times* (Nov. 20, 2016); http://www.nytimes.com/2016/11/20/business/media/how-fake-news-spreads.html

[20] Silverman, C. This analysis shows how viral fake election news stories outperformed real news on Facebook. *BuzzFeed* (Nov. 16, 2016); https://www.buzzfeed.com/craigsilverman/viral-fake-election-news-outperformed-real-news-on-facebook?utm_term=.xu3M8zonA#.xqbRqV1D8

[21] Kang, C. Fake news onslaught targets pizzeria as nest of child-trafficking. *The New York Times* (Nov. 21, 2016); http://www.nytimes.com/2016/11/21/technology/fact-check-this-pizzeria-is-not-a-child-trafficking-site.html

[22] Bender, B. and Hanna, A. Flynn under fire for fake news. *Politico* (Dec. 5, 2016); http://www.politico.com/story/2016/12/michael-flynn-conspiracy-pizzeria-trump-232227

[23] Jin, F., Dougherty, E., Saraf, P., Cao, Y., and Ramakrishnan, N. Epidemiological modeling of news and rumors on Twitter. In *Proceedings of the Seventh Workshop on Social Network Mining and Analysis*. ACM Press, New York, 2013, article no. 8.

[24] Kottasova, I. Facebook and Google to stop ads from appearing on fake news sites. *CNN* (Nov. 15, 2016); http://money.cnn.com/2016/11/15/technology/facebook-google-fake-news-presidential-election/index.html

[25] Heath, A. Facebook is going to use Snopes and other fact-checkers to combat and bury 'fake news.' *Business Insider* (Dec. 15, 2016); http://www.businessinsider.com/facebook-will-fact-check-label-fake-news-in-news-feed-2016-12

[26] Resnick, P., Kelly Garrett, R., Kriplean, T., Munson, S.A., and Jomini Stroud, N. Bursting your (filter) bubble: Strategies for promoting diverse exposure. In *Proceedings of the 2013 Conference on Computer Supported Cooperative Work* (San Antonio, TX, Feb. 23–27). ACM Press, New York, 2013, 95–100.

Periodical and Internet Sources Bibliography

Anthony Andrew, "The Great Digital-Age Swindle...and the Man Fighting Back," *Guardian*, May 17, 2017. https://www. theguardian.com/technology/2017/may/21/jonathan-taplin-interview-move-fast-break-things-facebook-google-amazon-dylan-scorsese.

Drake Baer, "The 'Filter Bubble' Explains Why Trump Won and You Didn't See It Coming," Science of Us, November 9, 2016. http://nymag.com/scienceofus/2016/11/how-facebook-and-the-filter-bubble-pushed-trump-to-victory.html.

Daphne Bramham, "Will Big Data Steer You to Decide B.C. Election Outcome?" *Vancouver Sun*, April 4, 2017. http://www.montrealgazette.com/opinion/columnists/daphne+bramham+will+data+steer+decide+election/13269218/story.html.

Cory Doctorow, "I've Created a Monster! And So Can You," Slate, May 22, 2017. http://www.slate.com/articles/technology/future_tense/2017/05/sci_fi_doesn_t_predict_the_future_it_influences_it.html.

Robson Fletcher, "In Search of 'James Galan': How Seemingly Fake Social Media Accounts Permeate Alberta Politics," CBC news, May 24, 2017. http://www.cbc.ca/beta/news/canada/calgary/fake-facebook-accounts-calgary-alberta-politics-1.4128312.

Nathalia Gjersoe, "Negativity Bias: Why Conservatives Are More Swayed by Threats Than Liberals," *Guardian*, May 26, 2017. https://www.theguardian.com/science/head-quarters/2017/may/26/negativity-bias-why-conservatives-are-more-swayed-by-threats-than-liberals?CMP=Share_iOSApp_Other.

Dirk Helbing, Bruno S. Frey, Gerd Gigerenzer, Ernst Hafen, Michael Hagner, Yvonne Hofstetter, Jeroen van den Hoven, Roberto V. Zicari, and Andrej Zwitter, "Will Democracy Survive Big Data and Artificial Intelligence?" *Scientific American*, February 25, 2017. https://www.scientificamerican.com/article/will-democracy-survive-big-data-and-artificial-intelligence/.

Paula Simons, "Travelling Hate Circus Staged Anti-Syrian Protest in Red Deer Based on Lie," *Edmonton Journal*, May 24, 2017. http://edmontonjournal.com/opinion/columnists/paula-simons-travelling-hate-circus-staged-anti-syrian-protest-in-red-deer-based-on-lie.

Matthew Wills, "Dada at 100, or, I Zimbra!" Jstor Daily, November 11, 2016. https://daily.jstor.org/dada-at-100-or-101-or/.

OPPOSING
VIEWPOINTS®
SERIES

CHAPTER 4

Is There Hope of Bursting Online Filter Bubbles?

Chapter Preface

What are the ethics of setting up and taking apart information filters? According to some users, it's the responsibility of service providers and website and social media corporate entities to lessen the echo chamber effect of filter bubbles. Others say that government should get involved and pass legislation that helps avoid this trap by limiting collection of personal information. What can be done to burst a filter bubble? Some people are discussing alternatives to generating filter bubbles and alternatives for improving people's access to a variety of viewpoints.

Facebook and other outlets that offer news items have taken heat for creating bubbles, particularly regarding the 2016 election. What is being done, if anything, to address this? The massively popular site has morphed into much more than its original design. Facebook was not set up to be in the business of news, so perhaps it doesn't have the same goals as traditional media outlets. But should it? What are the responsibilities and legal ramifications of social media sites through which users spread news and information? Is anyone legally liable for online curating turning into filter bubbles? Do social media users have any legal recourse for being kept from certain news or information sources? Overall, most sources agree that it's the individual's responsibility to look outside the bubble.

> *"Trending news stories, both fake and real, buy into what's called the attention economy, whereby 'if people pay attention to a certain topic, more information on that topic will be produced.'"*

Employ Critical Thinking to Detect False Stories

Nsikan Akpan

In the following viewpoint, Nsikan Akpan argues that while filter bubbles are widely regarded as a problem, blaming platforms like Facebook is misguided, since custom experiences are part of their design and are a large reason users like them. The author uses examples such as the Pizzagate conspiracy theory and the hysteria over potential cases of Ebola in the United States to illustrate that users follow high-drama stories. This feeds into the "attention economy," producing even more content on that topic. The end message is that readers should always question what they are reading, think critically, and look to a variety of information sources. Akpan is the digital science producer for PBS NewsHour.

"The Very Real Consequences of Fake News Stories and Why Your Brain Can't Ignore Them," by Nsikan Akpan, NewsHour Productions LLC., December 5, 2016. Reprinted by permission.

As you read, consider the following questions:

1. What news story is mentioned as the "cottage industry" for fake stories, according to the viewpoint?
2. What does the author cite as the most prevalent variety of fake news?
3. How can robots help filter fake news stories?

On Sunday afternoon, a 28-year-old man walked into a Washington, D.C. ping-pong bar and pizzeria. He was carrying an AR-15 assault rifle—hardly standard-issue hardware for a round of table tennis. He fired one or more shots, as people fled Comet Ping Pong, before surrendering to police officers. No one was injured.

Edgar Maddison Welch told police he had traveled from his home in Salisbury, N.C. to the nation's capital to investigate a pre-election conspiracy theory, wherein Democratic presidential nominee Hillary Clinton allegedly led a child-trafficking ring out of Comet Ping Pong.

A false claim started by, you guessed it, fake news.

Fake news, once confined to satire or the fringe bowels of the internet, has quickly become a contender for the most influential phrase of the year. Following Donald Trump's surprise election, story after story has questioned the role that fake news played in swaying voters—and for good reason. A BuzzFeed analysis found fake election news outperformed total engagement on Facebook when compared to the most popular election stories from 19 major news outlet combined. Facebook CEO Mark Zuckerberg described this allegation as "a pretty crazy idea" before ultimately announcing a move to deter misleading news. Later, Facebook and Google took steps to keep fake news sites from collecting revenue from their ad platforms.

To some degree, Zuckerberg's initial stance was warranted. A panel of experts told the NewsHour that it would be nearly impossible to prove that phony stories swayed the U.S. election in one direction or another, based on current research. On the flip side, they said incidents like the #Pizzagate shooting signify just one step in a long, dark trail of real world consequences caused by fake news—one that started well before this year. They argued that emerging technology may stem the tide of garbage news in the near future. And they highlighted one solution that already exists.

Before Pizzagate, Came Ebola

Fake news comes in many flavors, like satire or intentional hoaxes, but computer scientist Filippo Menczer said sensational news and social media campaigns filled with mistruths—like the PizzaGate story—started to surge on the internet around 2010.

"That is the first time that we started studying it actively, and at that time, we found several cases of websites that were publishing completely fake and fabricated news, purely for political propaganda," said Menczer, who designs algorithms to track political messaging as director of Indiana University's Center for Complex Networks and Systems Research.

Menczer recalled an example that occurred in 2010 during the special election to fill the vacancy created by the death of Massachusetts Senator Ted Kennedy. Researchers at Wellesley College found that, in the hours before the election, a Republican group from Iowa used thousands of Twitter bots to spread misinformation about the Democratic candidate Martha Coakley. At the time, search engines prioritized "real-time information" from social media platforms, so these fake posts topped search results just as people headed to the polls.

Six years ago, few fake news websites featured ads for their content, Menczer said. Their main goal was political gain. By his estimation, the cottage industry for phony stories appeared to take off during the 2014 Ebola crisis. The websites for places like National Report, which self identifies as political satire, began to resemble legitimate news sources. False stories on National Report like "Texas Town Quarantined After Family Of Five Test Positive

For The Ebola Virus" feature elements like author biographies and video shorts embedded in the page to give the feel of authenticity, Menczer said. Whether those attributes or the "satirical writing" mislead people is hard to say. But the Texas story, which lacks a disclaimer in the body of the text that clearly identifies it as satire, was shared more than 330,000 times on Facebook according to MuckRack's WhoShared algorithm.

Irrational fears of the Ebola virus in the U.S. arguably drove web interest in this fake news story, as it likely did for any number of legitimate articles written during the outbreak. When the dust settled, America notched four imported cases and one death during the entire course of the epidemic, while in contrast Africa experienced around 30,000 cases and 11,000 deaths.

Yet the American news machine had its share of media casualties during the Ebola crisis. One example involved Kaci Hickox, a Doctors Without Borders nurse who volunteered to treat people in West Africa.

Upon returning on a flight through Newark, she was quarantined for 80 hours by the New Jersey Department of Health and Gov. Chris Christie, despite showing no conclusive symptoms. Even after an Ebola test came back and she was released, Gov. Christie reportedly said Hickox may be "tested for that again, because sometimes it takes a little bit longer to make a definitive determination," and that "There's no question the woman is ill, the question is what is her illness."

From Hickox's perspective, the modern news cycle did the rest.

"The statements were completely untrue, but they were printed and published. Interviews with Chris Christie were playing on the news," Hickox told NewsHour. "It was another example of when you have a politician who really has access to say whatever they want, even though it was completely inaccurate."

The negative ramifications occurred immediately. As Hickox journeyed home to Maine, her landlord left a voicemail on her partner's cell phone, asking them to move out. "Before I left for

Sierra Leone, she was very supportive, and she told me how amazing it was that I had the skills to go help respond to the Ebola outbreak," Hickox recalled. "Then all of a sudden this woman doesn't want you to return home, even though I never had Ebola, I wasn't symptomatic and there was no reason for anyone to fear."

Those public fears ballooned when Maine Gov. Paul LePage followed in Christie's tracks and tried to enforce a similar quarantine. Maine police officers complained about fielding phone calls from concerned residents who had been duped by fake news articles. Hickox heard rumors from the police department about physical threats against her, and her partner ended up dropping out of nursing school because they wouldn't allow him to attend while he was living with her, she said. The couple opted to ultimately go on a widely publicized bike ride to, in essence, force a judge to make a decision about the quarantine, a point that was missed by the mainstream media, she said.

"The state hadn't met the burden of proof to say that I needed to be quarantined. No one really explained that," Hickox said. A Reuters headline at the time, for instance, read "Bike-riding nurse defies Ebola quarantine, on collision course with governor"—even though no court had issued an official quarantine at the time.

Hickox, who ultimately left Maine, said outside Christie and LePage, she wasn't sure who to blame for the unjustified hype around her story.

"Is it the media that causes public panic, or is it that we, the public, just desire drama and fear, and that therefore feeds into the media," Hickox asked.

Based on research, the answer is both, as Menczer detailed recently in an OpEd for The Conversation. Trending news stories, both fake and real, buy into what's called the attention economy, whereby "if people pay attention to a certain topic, more information on that topic will be produced."

Why Your Brain Loves Fake News

Tell me if you've heard this common refrain since the election: "If people were smarter, fake news wouldn't be a problem," or "Readers are responsible for telling fake news from the real stuff. Don't blame Facebook."

But to communications psychologist Dannagal Young, blaming readers for spreading fake news from a cognitive perspective is somewhat equivalent to blaming a baby for soiling itself. They can't help it.

This takeaway comes after a decade of studying how the human mind responds to political satire. Satire is arguably the most prevalent variety of fake news and arguably the best studied. The mental processing of satire is unique compared to other types of information, Young said, because it requires audience participation.

"So compared to what we see in traditional communication, there is this enhanced attention, enhanced interest and enhanced processing that happens," said Young, who works at the University of Delaware. "So things that you hear in the context of humor will be more on the top of your mind."

But here's where problem lies with fake news and the human mind. Our brains have a finite capacity for processing information and for remembering, so our minds make value judgments about what to keep. Humor tips the scales in favor of being remembered and recalled, even when counterarguments are strong.

"The special sauce of humor is that you might get people to entertain ideas of constructs that they otherwise might reject out of hand," she said, and this powerful mode of persuasion extends to sensational fake news as well. "When you have exposure to fake news or satire, or any content at all, as soon as those constructs have been accessed and brought into working memory, they are there. You can't un-think them."

This mental reflex may explain why caricature traits—"Al Gore is stiff and robotic" or "George W. Bush is dumb"—persist in the zeitgeist for so long despite being untrue, Young said.

These days, the trouble arises from people being unable to recognize irony in online satire, Young said. She offered the example of a recent Change.org petition—Allow Open Carry of Firearms at the Quicken Loans Arena during the RNC Convention in July. The petition was written as if real, and news outlets like USA Today assumed as much, but its gun control-supporting author was actually trying to portray what he viewed as hypocrisy from conservative politicians. Young argued spoken irony—think John Oliver—creates less confusion because it's easier to recognize the tones of intent.

How to Beat Fake News

So, what happens next in the wild west of phony tales? Some are looking to robots to save the day. For example, the verbal themes of satire are so distinctive, so salient, that linguists like Victoria Rubin can engineer machine-learning algorithms to filter this brand of fake news from legitimate articles.

"We were able to reach about 86 percent accuracy, which means definitely eight out of 10 would be pinpointed as satire," said Rubin, who studies information and media at the University of Western Ontario. These algorithms are trained to spot the hallmarks of satire, like extra-long sentences or unexpected juxtapositions of random people and places, locations.

These programs, however, still struggle when it comes to identifying the type of misinformation present in sensational news items. Their attempts at a deception detector yielded a 63 percent success rate, which is better than the human ability to spot lies— 54 percent on average—but not by much.

In recent weeks, many have called on Facebook to develop such programs or other methods to stop fake news, but Young said the social media platform had tried long before fake news became a mainstream problem.

A year and a half ago, Young said Facebook rolled out satire labeling for stories from satirical sources like The Onion. She said readers disliked this option because part of the allure of satire is getting momentarily swept up before realizing the story is a joke.

Next, Facebook tried a button in the right corner of posts that allowed readers to flag posts as fake, but then satirical content producers like The Daily Currant protested, based on research to be published by Young in an upcoming book in 2017. Facebook appeared to change how flagged stories were distributed, and referrals from Facebook to The Daily Currant dropped by 95 percent within a few months.

Though this crowdsourced option for reporting fake news still exists, Young said its influence on the distribution of stories into news feeds may have been supplanted by the "reaction emojis" that Facebook introduced in February. But she wonders if a "Ha-ha" or "sad" emoji carries the weight in crowdsourcing remarks about misinformative news.

Both she and Menczer also question whether crowdsourcing is the best path to defeating fake news on social media.

"I have been a huge advocate of digital technologies as an inherently democratizing medium that's going to change everything. Now I'm like, 'Oh my God, we have destroyed ourselves,'" Young said, somewhat in jest.

Since the election, many have tossed blame on Facebook for creating "filter bubbles" or "echo chambers" in users' news feed. But this notion rings hollow because these platforms are designed to cater to a people's choices. These decisions, Young said, are driven by confirmation bias and motivated reasoning. In other words, people share articles after reading only the headline, because they want to think they're right, she said. She votes for bringing back human gatekeepers to tailor trending news and to prevent fake stories from running amok.

Menczer recommended that social media users who want to avoid echo chambers should follow moderate news sources or organizations that don't necessarily match their most intimate viewpoints. Or, "don't unfollow people just because they post something you disagree with," he said. "Unfollowing is one of the most efficient techniques to put yourself inside an echo chamber."

Having lived through the consequences of such public behavior, Hickox is now cautious about how she views others in the news.

"I would encourage people to always be questioning whether they're only getting part of a story," Hickox said. "To make snap judgments that lead to fear and to discrimination against someone is not the right way, and will not get us anywhere."

> "*There is no reason to worry about pre-selected personalisation leading to filter bubble problems, briefly put, because the technology is still insufficient.*"

There Is No Need to Be Concerned About Online Filter Bubbles

Frederik J. Zuiderveen Borgesius, Damian Trilling, Judith Möller, Balázs Bodó, Claes H. de Vreese, and Natali Helberger

In the following viewpoint, Frederik J. Zuiderveen Borgesius, Damian Trilling, Judith Möller, Balázs Bodó, Claes H. de Vreese, and Natali Helberger argue that there is little evidence that filter bubbles are something we should worry about. In their study, the authors synthesize empirical research on the extent and effects of self-selected personalization, where people actively choose which content they receive, and pre-selected personalization, where algorithms personalize content for users without any deliberate user choice. They caution that we should not lead with panic or fear when responding to newly emerging issues of the digital age. The authors all are researchers affiliated with the University of Amsterdam.

As you read, consider the following questions:

1. What is the concept of the "daily me"?
2. What percentage of Google searches differ because of personalization?
3. What is one example of a force that can counteract the effects of personalization?

Self-Selected and Pre-Selected Personalised Communications

In his book *Being Digital*, Negroponte (1995) discussed the idea of the "daily me." He suggested that people would soon be able to choose their own personalised media experiences:

> Imagine a future in which your interface agent can read every newswire and newspaper and catch every TV and radio broadcast on the planet, and then construct a personalized summary. This kind of newspaper is printed in an edition of one. (Negroponte, 1995, p. 153)

Others worry that people can lock themselves in information cocoons or echo chambers. For instance, somebody might read only left-leaning blogs and websites, listen only to left-leaning radio, and watch only left-leaning television. Pariser coined the term "filter bubble," "a unique universe of information for each of us" (Pariser, 2011, p. 9). For example, a personalised news website could give more prominence to conservative media items, based on the inferred political interests of the user. When they form their political ideas, users of such personalised services may encounter fewer opinions or political arguments.

We distinguish between two main types of personalization: *self-selected personalisation* and *pre-selected personalisation*. Others have used different terms to describe similar phenomena: For instance, self-selected personalisation could also be called "explicit personalisation," and pre-selected personalisation could be called "implicit personalisation" (Thurman & Schifferes 2012; see also Treiblmaier, Madlberger, Knotzer, & Pollach, 2004).

Self-selected personalisation concerns situations in which people *choose* to encounter like-minded opinions exclusively. For example, a person who opposes immigration might want to avoid information that specifies how much a country has gained due to immigration, while paying a lot of attention to news stories about problems related to immigration. People tend to avoid information that challenges their point of view, for example by avoiding news outlets that often feature editorials that favour an opposing political camp. In communication science, this phenomenon is conceptualised as *selective exposure* (e.g. Stroud, 2011).

Pre-selected personalisation concerns personalisation driven by websites, advertisers, or other actors, often *without* the user's deliberate choice, input, knowledge or consent. Concerns about pre-selected personalisation are often summarised with the term 'filter bubble' (Pariser, 2011).

Pre-selected personalisation may be chosen by the user, or not. For instance, some people may realise that Facebook personalises the content in its newsfeed. If these people explicitly use Facebook to see the curated, pre-selected collection of news about "friends," the newsfeed is an example of chosen pre-selected personalisation. Other people, however, may not realise that the newsfeed on Facebook is personalised; those people do not explicitly choose pre-selected personalisation.

Concerns Around Personalised Communication

Below, we summarise the main concerns regarding personalisation that have been brought forward in policy and scholarly circles. We discuss the effects of personalisation on democracy, the role of new gatekeepers and influencers of public opinion, autonomy-related concerns, the lack of transparency around personalisation, and the possibilities for social sorting. Examining the privacy implications of the massive collection of user data that is often involved in personalisation lies beyond the scope of this paper (for privacy implications of personalised services, see Zuiderveen Borgesius, 2015).

Effects on Democracy

Many worry about the effects that personalised communication could have on democracy. When the High Level Expert Group on Media Diversity and Pluralism commented on personalisation strategies in the media, one of its main concerns was that people would encounter fewer opinions, which could have a negative effect on the public sphere and the democratic opinion forming process (Vīķe-Freiberga et al., 2013). In a similar vein, the Council of Europe (2012, Appendix, Section I, paragraph 2) warned that the ordering and ranking of information in the context of search engines can affect information access and the diversity of information people are exposed to.

The concerns of the Expert Group echo arguments made in the scholarly debate, including those by Sunstein (to whom the group refers) (Vīķe-Freiberga et al., 2013). Sunstein discusses risks of too much personalisation. He mainly addresses self-selected personalisation: people locking themselves in "information cocoons," which he describes as "communication universes in which we hear only what we choose and only what comforts us and pleases us" (Sunstein 2006, p. 9). To give a current example: somebody might self-select personalisation by following people on Twitter who hold like-minded opinions.

Sunstein discusses two risks of personalisation. First, in a democratic society people need to come across opinions that differ from their own opinions, to develop themselves fully. Otherwise, people might enter a spiral of attitudinal reinforcement and drift towards more extreme viewpoints (Sunstein 2002, p. 9). This is a point also shared by the Expert Group: "The concern is people forgetting that alternatives do exist and hence becoming encapsulated in rigid positions that may hinder consensus-building in society" (Vīķe-Freiberga et al., 2013, pp. 27-28). Sunstein warns that "unplanned, unanticipated encounters are central to democracy itself" (2002, p. 9).

Second, if people locked themselves in their own information cocoons, they might have fewer common experiences. Sunstein says a diverse democratic society needs shared experiences as "social glue" (2002, p. 9). The Habermasian understanding of the public sphere, in which societally relevant ideas are formulated, negotiated and distributed, and in the process the ruling authorities' actions are kept under control and guided (Habermas, 1989), still serves as an important point of reference, despite the extensive critique this idea rightly received.

New Gatekeepers and Influencers of Public Opinion
In the public policy discourse, much attention is given to search engines, app stores, and social network sites as new gatekeepers and influencers of public opinion (see e.g., European Commission, 2013, p. 13; Vīķe-Freiberga et al., 2013). There is a long tradition in media law and policy of regulating gatekeeper control, because such control can threaten the realisation of important public policy goals, such as media diversity, public debate and competition on the marketplace of ideas.

However, the new information intermediaries, such as providers of search engines, social network sites, and app stores, differ in many respects from the more traditional gatekeeper categories, like the old press barons and controllers of content and infrastructure. One of the most important differences is the set of mechanisms used to exercise gatekeeping control which, in the case of the new intermediaries, are often related to interaction with users, the amount of knowledge and control they have over the user base, and exposure to diverse information (Helberger, Kleinen-von Königslöw, & Van der Noll, 2015).

An experiment in which Facebook persuaded its users to vote in the US election demonstrates the power of new opinion influencers well. The "results suggest that the Facebook social message increased turnout directly by about 60,000 voters and indirectly through social contagion by another 280,000 voters, for a total of 340,000 additional votes. That represents about 0.14% of the voting age population of about 236 million in 2010" (Bond, Fariss, Jones, Kramer, Marlow, Settle, & Fowler, 2012, p.

1). Because of the potential power of gatekeepers, various scholars call for meaningful transparency regarding their algorithms and their profiling practices (Hildebrandt & Gutwirth, 2008; Pasquale, 2015; Bozdag, 2015).

Autonomy-Related Concerns

Personalised communication may also restrict people's autonomy, according to some authors (e.g. Zarsky 2002, p. 42). In brief, people's opinions might be steered by personalised media, while they are not aware of being influenced.

However, personalisation, at least self-selected personalisation, could also enhance people's autonomy, because people can express which content they wish to receive. In contrast, in the traditional mass media situation, the editor determines which content is presented in which form. In other words, personalisation strategies can also have an empowering effect on users. In fact, pre-selected personalisation can also be used to help users make more diverse choices (Helberger, 2011).

Lack of Transparency

Another prominent item on the media policy agenda is the lack of transparency regarding pre-selected personalisation. The lack of transparency could affect the way people respond to personalised messages (Vīķe-Freiberga et al., 2013), and could make it harder for regulators to monitor the media sector. If people do not realise they see pre-selected content, they might think they see the same content as everybody else.

The Council of Europe seems to suggest that transparency about the search algorithm can help to promote media diversity and information access, and help to mitigate the filter bubble risk (Council of Europe, 2012, paragraph 7 and Appendix, Section 1, paragraph 4). Transparency in itself may not promote diversity of supply and exposure, but transparency is a necessary, albeit insufficient condition to detect problems with diversity. It is also unclear whether information about the way search engines work can cause people to choose more diverse content or can help people to avoid being trapped in a filter bubble. However, transparency about personalisation is at least essential to inform the policy discussions.

Social Sorting

Topics that received little attention in the public policy discourse on personalised communication are social sorting and discriminatory practices. Scholars have paid more attention to these topics. Social sorting involves, in Lyon's words, "obtain[ing] personal and group data in order to classify people and populations according to varying criteria, to determine who should be targeted for special treatment, suspicion, eligibility, inclusion, access, and so on" (Lyon, 2003, p. 20). In particular, profiling and classification in one domain (for example in advertising) may outgrow its original context and define other domains of our life (Turow, 2011). Social sorting, thus, "may further erode the tolerance and mutual dependence between diverse groups that enable a society to work" (Turow, 2011, p. 196).

Conclusion

In public policy and academic discourse, personalised communication is regarded with much concern. Much of the existing public policy discourse makes little reference to empirical evidence, leaving unclear to what extent concerns are justified, exaggerated, or underestimated.

Empirical research into the extent of personalised communication, and its effects on access to diverse information, can serve as a reality check. Empirical research can help to adjust the priorities in public policy, and to identify areas in which we simply do not know enough to make any conclusive policy statements. Below, we focus on empirical evidence of the spread of personalised news services and its likely effects on political polarisation and political information.

How Common Is Personalisation?

Prevalence of Self-Selected Personalisation

Selectively using information that matches pre-existing beliefs is human. People tend to avoid media content that conflicts with their beliefs (Festinger, 1957). The first data on this were collected during a US election campaign in 1940: Democrats were more likely to be exposed to the Democratic Campaign, and Republicans to the Republican campaign (Lazarsfeld, Berelson, & Gaudet, 1944). Many European countries have known a strong party press until the first half of the 20th century, with people being exposed to mainly like-minded information (Hallin & Mancini, 2004). A prime example is the period of pillarisation (*verzuiling*) in the Netherlands, where Catholics were commonly assumed to read a Catholic newspaper, to join a Catholic sports club, and to listen to Catholic radio. Left-voting labour workers had their own pillar, as did protestants (Lijphart, 1968; Wijfjes, 2004). Although the premise that the cleavages were that rigid has been challenged somewhat (Bax, 1988; Blom & Talsma, 2000), being exposed to like-minded content was pretty likely.

Nevertheless, in a literature review from as early as 1967, Sears and Freedman (1967) contest the idea that selective exposure occurs because of cognitive dissonance. In the decades that followed, interest in the topic was lost, in part because media choice was limited to few TV channels and newspapers, rendering the mechanism somewhat irrelevant. Once the choice grew with the advent of cable TV and the internet, the topic gained renewed scholarly interest.

Whereas it is trivial to show that the audience of partisan media outlets in general is partisan as well, this does not have to be problematic from a normative point of view. It is insufficient to look at usage of isolated media outlets, because those who use a lot of partisan information *also* use an above-average amount of mainstream news (e.g., Bimber & Davis, 2003; Trilling & Schoenbach, 2015; Zaller, 1992). Furthermore, at least in Europe, most people by far still get their news via traditional sources, most notably public-service television (Blekesaune, Elvestad, & Aalberg, 2012; Trilling & Schoenbach 2013a, 2013b, 2015). The fact that fewer people watch mainstream TV news and read newspapers does not mean that people massively turn to alternative specialist outlets; most online outlets with a substantial reach are spin-offs of traditional media. Thus, those who use extremely partisan outlets are mostly exposed to moderate ideas as well. If there are echo chambers, the walls are pretty porous. Therefore, Garret distinguishes between *selective exposure* and *selective avoidance*: while there is some evidence that people *select* information they agree with, it is much less certain whether people actually *avoid* possibly conflicting information (Garret, 2009a, 2009b; Garret, Carnahan, & Lynch, 2011).

In summary, people self-select information they agree with, but the importance of this might not be as dramatic as often suggested, because even if people self-select consonant content, they may well be confronted with conflicting content as well.

Prevalence of Pre-Selected Personalisation

In contrast to self-selected personalisation, pre-selected personalisation is not a result of a user's direct choice—but of a choice that is determined by algorithms. This is commonly known from recommendations on online shopping sites or on YouTube (O'Callaghan, Greene, Conway, Carthy, & Cunningham, 2013) and in the context of online search results (Van Hoboken, 2012; Dillahunt, Brooks, & Gulati, 2015). It is debatable how common and far-reaching pre-selected personalisation is. For example, there is some evidence that 11% of Google searches differ due to personalisation (Hannak, Sapiezynski, Molavi Kakhki, Krishnamurthy, Lazer, Mislove, & Wilson, 2013). Whether this 11% is a high percentage or not is impossible to tell as we lack the adequate benchmarks.

On news sites, algorithmic personalisation is still less prevalent. People generally have the choice whether they want their online news to be personalised or not. Additionally, people who choose pre-selected personalisation are more likely to use an above-average amount of general-interest news as well (Beam & Kosicki, 2014), and to encounter messages that are not in line with their own ideas (Beam, 2013). However, as personalisation on news websites is still in its infancy, in the future the effects may be different (Thurman & Schifferes, 2012; Turow, 2011).

While personalisation features on news sites themselves are not common yet, de facto algorithmic personalisation can arise on two other layers: news aggregators and social networks. Purely algorithmic news aggregators like Google News have mostly failed to become a major news source for a large audience, but more and more traffic to news sites goes via social media sites, which use a blend of algorithmic and human recommendations to define the supply of news items for the individual.

Social media sites can lead to two sources of personalisation. First, although people connect with different types of contacts (friends, family, colleagues etc.) on such sites, many people might mostly connect to people who resemble them. If someone's network is rather homogeneous, this means that the content shared by someone's contacts may be in line with the person's preferences as well. This argument is based on the assumption that people only share content they agree with—an assumption that has been challenged by some (Barbera, Jost, Nagler, Tucker, & Bonneau, 2015; Morgan, Shafiq, & Lampe, 2013).

Second, on some sites, most prominently on Facebook, an opaque algorithm determines what content is shown in a user's newsfeed. A recent study suggests that the influence of this algorithm is lower than the influence of the user's choices (Bakshy, Messing, & Adamic, 2015). However, the validity of this study is debated among social science scholars and beyond (Lumb, 2015).

In sum, it looks as if either personalisation is still in its infancy on news sites, or we have too little empirical evidence on what is actually happening in this domain. More independent research is necessary.

What Are the Effects of Personalisation?

An even harder question concerns the long-term effects of personalisation. Does personalised content really influence people? Does, or could, personalisation really harm democracy? While the effects of self-selected personalisation on democracy have been studied in a number of experiments and surveys, the effects of pre-selected personalisation have not been investigated in a comprehensive academic study so far.

In general, we can expect effects of selective exposure or selective avoidance on two different variables that are relevant in democratic societies: political polarisation and political knowledge.

Polarisation as a Consequence of Self-Selected Personalisation

Numerous scholars of political communication have studied the effects of a selective media diet on democratic societies. Most of these studies are concerned with one potential consequence of selective exposure that might be harmful to democratic societies: partisan polarisation.

According to this line of research, people who are repeatedly exposed to biased information that favours a particular political standpoint that is close to their own will eventually develop more extreme positions and be less tolerant with regard to opposite points of view. Empirical evidence from the US supports this argument. For example, Stroud (2010) used representative American election survey data to show that Americans who adopt a homogenous partisan news diet become more extreme in their views during the campaign. Similar effects of self-selective exposure to partisan news on polarisation were also found in experimental settings (e.g. Knobloch-Westerwick & Meng, 2011).

To understand the importance of cross-cutting information in a democracy, Price, Cappella, and Nir (2002) investigated the effects of being exposed to information in the mass media that contradicts existing attitudes and beliefs. They found that people who regularly encounter diverse opinions in the media are not only better able to provide reasons for their own political choices; they also have a better understanding of what motivates the perspective of others.

The effect of personalised news on polarisation is conditional on the political system. Most of the research on the effect of polarisation stems from the US, which is characterised by a bipolar political system, in which the issue of polarisation is substantially different than, for example, in the Dutch political system where more than ten parties compete with each other (e.g., Trilling, Van Klingeren, & Tsfati, 2016). This difference between political systems must be kept in mind when discussing the effects of personalisation.

Political Learning, as Impacted by Self-Selected Personalisation

While there is a growing body of studies providing evidence that selective exposure is related to polarisation, evidence on the effect of selective exposure or selective avoidance on knowledge gains is scarce. Yet, there is a strong theoretical link between political knowledge and self-selected personalised communication.

First, many media users take advantage of the abundance of media outlets to avoid political information altogether. Hence, these users lose an important information source to form political opinions (Prior, 2007). Second, if media users select political information that is attractive to them, they will be better motivated to process the information they encounter.

Hence, personalisation might lead to knowledge gaps in society: News avoiders know little. Those who self-select political news learn more from the news. This holds in particular for online news sources where users can choose news they are interested in (Kenski & Stroud, 2006). However, the effects of self-selection of news on polarisation and political knowledge are—like most media effects—small. Additionally, the effect of a personalised and selective news menu is different for each individual, and many people are not affected (Valkenburg & Peter, 2013). The fact that the relationships introduced above are statistically significant means that there is convincing empirical proof that selective exposure to news and polarisation and differential knowledge gains are related. Yet, the fact that the effect is small means that selective exposure to news explains only a small fraction of the variance in political attitudes and political knowledge we find in democratic societies.

One of the reasons for the small effect is that hardly anyone lives in an absolute information cocoon, as mentioned previously. In the current fragmented media landscape, people can access an abundance of news sources. In addition, we often get information about current events through conversations with colleagues, friends, or family members. In such conversations people may be introduced to news items, or to different perspectives. Cross-cutting conversations about politics also can occur online, mostly in an environment that does not usually deal with political information, like an online hobby group (Wojcieszak & Mutz, 2009).

Effects of Pre-Selected Personalisation

Empirical research into the long-term effects of pre-selected personalisation is scarce (see Van Hoboken, 2012). The lack of empirical evidence can be partly explained by the fact that algorithms which automatically pre-select news items for individual users have only been developed in the past few years.

It is, however, possible that potential effects of pre-selected personalisation are in line with effects of self-selected personalisation. Being repeatedly exposed to the same news frame, for example, may lead to reinforcing framing effects (Lecheler & De Vreese, 2011). Potentially, algorithms that favour news items framing events in a perspective close to the reader's point of view will lead to a more polarised society. One of the first studies of news personalisation using search behaviour and social media as point of departure indeed found polarising effects, while also demonstrating an increase in cross-cutting exposure through social media (Flaxman, Goel, & Rao, 2014).

With regard to systematic gaps of knowledge about current events, pre-selected personalisation might contribute to social sorting, as explained above. If algorithms are programmed to favour news items that cover only a small set of topics that users are assumed to be interested in, users will not be exposed to information on many other topics that are important for society at large. As interest in news and politics correlates with higher education and higher social economic status, this could lead to a divided citizenry.

Moreover, commercial news providers gain power because they can control the algorithm. For example, a recent experiment carried out by Facebook shows that they were able to influence people's emotions by manipulating content. The experiment involved manipulating the selection of user messages ('posts') that 689,003 users saw in their newsfeeds. "When positive expressions were reduced, people produced fewer positive posts and more negative posts; when negative expressions were reduced, the opposite pattern occurred" (Kramer, Guillory & Hancock, 2014, p. 1). Hence, Facebook succeeded in influencing the emotions of users. However, the effects were rather small. In another study, the effects appeared to be stronger: Epstein and Robertson (2015) claim that differences in Google search results can shift voting preferences of undecided voters by 20%.

As outlined in a previous section, news users have always limited their exposure to specific news items themselves: a process of self-selected personalisation. Perhaps pre-selected personalisation by algorithms merely anticipates choices that news users would have made themselves?

Even if it were true that personalisation could influence people deeply, would the many possibilities to broaden one's horizon outweigh the effects of personalisation? For example, the web offers many ways to encounter unexpected content.

The effects of personalisation may be counteracted by other forces. For example, people who self-select content on some blogs and encounter a lot of pre-selected content on their Facebook newsfeed may still be avid users of non-personalised news sites as well.

Another reason to doubt whether there is a big risk that personalised content will steer people's worldview is that current personalisation technologies may be insufficient. For instance, with targeted online advertising (behavioural targeting) the click-through rate on ads is around 0.1% to 0.5% (e.g. Chaffey, 2015). This suggests that algorithms of companies do not predict people's interests very accurately. After all, around 999 out of 1,000 people do not click on ads—perhaps the ads do not appeal to the interests of most people. On the other hand, the low click-through rate on ads could perhaps be explained by scepticism towards advertising rather than by bad personalisation.

In sum, there is no reason to worry about pre-selected personalisation leading to filter bubble problems, briefly put, because the technology is still insufficient. With technological developments, however, problems may arise. As Hildebrandt notes, pre-selected personalisation could be seen as an early example of ambient intelligence: technology that senses and anticipates people's behaviour in order to adapt the environment to their inferred needs (Hildebrandt, 2010). Consequently, algorithmic accountability through transparency becomes more and more important as the technology develops (Diakopoulos, 2014).

References

Bakshy, E., Messing, S., & Adamic, L. (2015). Exposure to ideologically diverse news and opinion on Facebook. *Science, 58*(4), 707–731.

Barbera, P., Jost, J. T., Nagler, J., Tucker, J. A., & Bonneau, R. (2015). Tweeting from left to right: Is online political communication more than an echo chamber? *Psychological Science*, Advance online publication.

Bax, E.H. (1988). *Modernization and cleavage in Dutch society. A study of long term economic and social change*. PhD Dissertation, Rijksuniversteit Groningen, Netherlands.

Beam, M. A. (2013). Automating the news: How personalized news recommender system design choices impact news reception. *Communication Research, 14*, 1019-1041

Beam, M. A., & Kosicki, G. M. (2014). Personalized news portals: Filtering systems and increased news exposure. *Journalism & Mass Communication Quarterly, 91*(1), 59–77.

Bimber, B., & Davis, R. (2003). *Campaigning online: The Internet in U.S. elections*. New York: Oxford University Press.

Blekesaune, A., Elvestad, E., & Aalberg, T. (2012). Tuning out the world of news and current affairs: An empirical study of Europe's disconnected citizens. *European Sociological Review, 28*(1), 110–126.

Blom, C.H., & Talsma, J. (ed.) (2000). *De verzuiling voorbij. Godsdienst, stand en natie in de lange negentiende eeuw.* Amsterdam, Netherlands: Het Spinhuis.

Bond, R. M., Fariss, C. J., Jones, J. J., Kramer, A. D., Marlow, C., Settle, J. E., & Fowler, J. H. (2012). A 61-million-person experiment in social influence and political mobilization. *Nature, 489*(7415), 295-298.

Bozdag, E. (2015), *Bursting the Filter Bubble: Democracy, Design, and Ethics.* Delft University of Technology, PhD thesis.

Chaffey Chaffey, D. (2015, April). Display advertising clickthrough rates. *Smart Insights.* Retrieved from http://www.smartinsights.com/internet-advertising/internet-advertising-a...

Cohen, S. (1973). *Folk devils and moral panics the creation of the Mods and Rockers.* St Albans: Paladin.

Council of Europe, Recommendation CM/Rec(2012)3 of the Committee of Ministers to member States on the protection of human rights with regard to search engines, adopted by the Committee of Ministers on 4 April 2012.

Diakopoulos, N. (2014). Algorithmic accountability. Journalistic investigation of computational power structures. Digital Journalism, 3, 398–415. http://doi.org/10.1080/21670811.2014.976411

Epstein, R., & Robertson, R. E. (2015). The search engine manipulation effect (SEME) and its possible impact on the outcomes of elections. *Proceedings of the National Academy of Sciences, 112*(33), E4512–E4521.

European Commission (2013). 'Preparing for a Fully Converged Audiovisual World: Growth, Creation and Values (Green Paper) Brussels, COM(2013) 231 final' (24 March 2013) https://ec.europa.eu/digital-agenda/sites/digital-agenda/files/convergen... accessed on 29 July 2015, p. 14.

Festinger, L. (1957). *A theory of cognitive dissonance.* Stanford, CA: Stanford University Press.

Flaxman, S. R., Goel, S., & Rao, J. M. (2014). Filter bubbles, echo chambers, and online news consumption. Retrieved from https://5harad.com/papers/bubbles.pdf

Gitlin, T. (1998). Public spheres or public sphericules. In T. Liebes & J. Curran (Eds.), Media, ritual and identity (pp. 168–174). London: Routledge.

Garrett, R. K. (2009). Echo chambers online?: Politically motivated selective exposure among Internet news users. *Journal of Computer-Mediated Communication, 14*(2), 265–285.

Garrett, R. K. (2009). Politically motivated reinforcement seeking: Reframing the selective exposure debate. *Journal of Communication, 59*(4), 676–699.

Garrett, R. K., Carnahan, D., & Lynch, E. K. (2011). A turn toward avoidance? Selective exposure to online political information, 2004–2008. *Political Behavior, 35*(1), 113–134.

Gutwirth, S. & Hildebrandt, M. eds. (2008). *Profiling the European Citizen.* Dordrecht: Springer 2008.

Habermas, J (1989). *The structural transformation of the public sphere: An inquiry into a category of bourgeois society.* Cambridge, MA: MIT Press.

Hallin, D. C., & Mancini, P. (2004). *Comparing Media Systems*. Cambridge, UK: Cambridge University Press.

Hannak, A., Sapiezynski, P., Molavi Kakhki, A., Krishnamurthy, B., Lazer, D., Mislove, A., & Wilson, C. (2013). Measuring personalization of web search. In *Proceedings of the 22Nd International Conference on World Wide Web* (pp. 527–538). Geneva, Switzerland: International World Wide Web Conferences Steering Committee.

Helberger, N. (2011). Diversity by design. *Journal of Information Policy, 1*, 441–469.

Helberger, N., Kleinen-Von Königslöw, K. and Van der Noll, R. (2015). Regulating the new information intermediaries as gatekeepers of information diversity, *info 17*(6), p. 50-71.

Hildebrandt, M. (2010). Privacy en identiteit in slimme omgevingen. *Computerrecht, 6*, 172-182.

Kenski, K., & Stroud, N. J. (2006). Connections between Internet use and political efficacy, knowledge, and participation. *Journal of Broadcasting & Electronic Media, 50*(2), 173–192.

Kim, J., Kim, J., & Seo, M. (2014). Toward a person × situation model of selective exposure: Repressors, sensitizers, and choice of online news on financial crisis. *Journal Of Media Psychology: Theories, Methods, And Applications, 26*(2), 59-69.

Knobloch-Westerwick, S., & Meng, J. (2011). Reinforcement of the Political Self Through Selective Exposure to Political Messages. *Journal of Communication, 61*(2), 349–368.

Kramer, A. D., Guillory, J. E., & Hancock, J. T. (2014). Experimental evidence of massive-scale emotional contagion through social networks. *Proceedings of the National Academy of Sciences, 111*(24), 8788-8790.

Lazarsfeld, P. F., Berelson, B., & Gaudet, H. (1944). *The people's choice: How the voter makes up his mind in a presidential campaign*. New York: Columbia University Press.

Lecheler, S., & de Vreese, C. H. (2011). Getting real: The duration of framing effects. *Journal of Communication, 61*(5), 959-983.

Lijphart, A. (1968). *Verzuiling, pacificatie en kentering in de Nederlandse politiek*. Amsterdam: De Bussy.

Lumb, D. (2015). Why scientists are upset about the Facebook Filter Bubble story. Retrieved from: http://www.fastcompany.com/3046111/fast-feed/why-scientists-are-upset-ov...

Lyon, D. (2003). Surveillance as social sorting: Computer codes and mobile bodies. In D. Lyon (ed.) *Surveillance as social sorting: Privacy, risk and automated discrimination* (pp. 13–30). New York, NY: Routledge.

Morgan, J. S., Shafiq, M. Z., & Lampe, C. (2013). Is news sharing on Twitter ideologically biased ? In *Proceedings of the 2013 conference on Computer supported cooperative work* (pp. 887–897). ACM.

Negroponte, N. (1995). *Being digital*. New York, NY: Knopf.

O'Callaghan, D., Greene, D., Conway, M., Carthy, J., & Cunningham, P. (2013). The extreme right filter bubble. *arXiv preprint arXiv:1308.6149*.

Pariser, E. (2011). *The filter bubble: What the Internet is hiding from you*. New York, NY: Penguin.

Pasquale F (2015). *The black box society: The secret algorithms that control money and information*. Cambridge: Harvard University Press.

Price, V., Cappella, J. N., & Nir, L. (2002). Does disagreement contribute to more deliberative opinion? *Political Communication, 19*(1), 95-112.

Prior, M. (2007). *Post-broadcast democracy: How media choice increases inequality in political involvement and polarizes elections.* Cambridge, UK: Cambridge University Press.

Sears, D. O., & Freedman, J. L. (1967). Selective exposure to information: A critical review. *Public Opinion Quarterly, 31*(2), 194–213.

Stroud, N. J. (2010). Polarization and partisan selective exposure. *Journal of Communication, 60*(3), 556–576.

Stroud, N. J. (2011). Niche news: The politics of news choice. Oxford University Press.

Sunstein, C. R. (2002). *Republic.com.* Princeton, NJ: Princeton University Press.

Sunstein C. R. (2006). *Infotopia: How many minds produce knowledge.* New York, NY: Oxford University Press

Dillahunt, T. R., Brooks, C. A., & Gulati, S. (2015, April). Detecting and Visualizing Filter Bubbles in Google and Bing. In *Proceedings of the 33rd Annual ACM Conference Extended Abstracts on Human Factors in Computing Systems* (pp. 1851-1856). ACM.

Thurman, N., & Schifferes, S. (2012). The future of personalization at news websites: Lessons from a longitudinal study. *Journalism Studies, 13*(5-6), 775-790.

Treiblmaier, H., Madlberger, M., Knotzer, N., & Pollach, I. (2004, January). Evaluating personalization and customization from an ethical point of view: an empirical study. In *System Sciences, 2004. Proceedings of the 37th Annual Hawaii International Conference on System Sciences* (pp. 10-pp). IEEE.

Trilling, D., & Schoenbach, K. (2013a). Patterns of news consumption in Austria: How fragmented are they? *International Journal of Communication, 7*, 929–953.

Trilling, D., & Schoenbach, K. (2013b). Skipping current affairs: The non-users of online and offline news. *European Journal of Communication, 28*(1), 35–51.

Trilling, D., & Schoenbach, K. (2015). Investigating people's news diets: How online news users use offline news. Communications: *The European Journal of Communication Research, 40*(1), 67–91.

Trilling, D., Van Klingeren, M., & Tsfati, Y. (2016). Selective exposure, political polarization, and possible mediators: Evidence from the Netherlands. *International Journal of Public Opinion Research*, online first. doi:10.1093/ijpor/edw003

Turow, J. (2011). The daily you: How the new advertising industry is defining your identity and your worth. New Haven, CT: Yale University Press.

Van Hoboken, J. V. J. (2012). *Search engine freedom: on the implications of the right to freedom of expression for the legal governance of search engines.* Alphen aan den Rijn, Netherlands: Kluwer Law International.

Valkenburg, P. & Peter, J.(2013). The differential susceptibility to media effects model. *Journal of Communication 63*(2), 221–243.

Vīķe-Freiberga, V., Däubler-Gmelin, H., Hammersley, B., Pessoa Maduro, L.M.P. (2013). *A free and pluralistic media to sustain European democracy.* Retrieved from http://ec.europa.eu/digital-agenda/sites/digital-agenda/files/HLG%20Fina...

Wojcieszak, M. E., & Mutz, D. C. (2009). Online groups and political discourse: Do online discussion spaces facilitate exposure to political disagreement? Journal of Communication, 59(1), 40–56.

Wijfjes, H. (ed.) (2004). *Journalistiek in Nederland. Beroep, cultuur en organisatie 1850-2000.* Amsterdam, Netherlands: Boom.

Zaller, J. R. (1992). *The nature and origins of mass opinion.* Cambridge, UK: Cambridge University Press.

Zarsky, T. Z. (2002). Mine your own business: making the case for the implications of the data mining of personal information in the forum of public opinion. *Yale Journal of Law and Technology* 5, 1–56.

Zuiderveen Borgesius, F.J. (2015). *Improving privacy protection in the area of behavioural targeting,* Alphen aan den Rijn, Netherlands: Kluwer Law International.

> "There's a strong argument that
> mainstream news only ever
> really represented the concerns
> of white, middle-class men, and
> of course it used to be much
> harder to consciously seek out
> alternative perspectives."

The Internet Offers a Host of Content Outside Our Bubbles

Jonathan Stray

In the following viewpoint, Jonathan Stray argues that online filter bubbles are nothing to panic about. The author observes how information filters in traditional news media have always served to control readers' access to news about current events and how information filters in social media are different. Still, he contends, digital technology makes it easier than ever before to expose ourselves to different viewpoints and a broader variety of content. The author suggests five new tactics to try in an effort to improve content delivery and quell the fear of filter bubbles. Stray teaches computational journalism at Columbia University and leads the Overview Project for the Associated Press.

As you read, consider the following questions:

1. Whose TED talk gave rise to the concept of online filter bubbles?
2. What does Facebook's link-sharing study reveal?
3. Why won't the elimination of filter bubbles solve the polarization of American politics, according to the author?

The filter bubble is a name for an anxiety—the worry that our personalized interfaces to the Internet will end up telling us only what we want to hear, hiding everything unpleasant but important. It's a fabulous topic of debate, because it's both significant and marvelously ill-defined. But to get beyond arguing, we're going to need to actually do something. I have five proposals.

If you're not familiar with the filter bubble argument, start with Eli Pariser's TED talk. The basic idea is this: All of us now depend on algorithmic personalization and recommendation, such as Google's personalized results and the Facebook news feed which decides for us whose updates we see. But if these individually-tailored filters are successful in giving us only what we want—as measured by what we click on or "like"—then maybe they'll remove all the points of view we disagree with, all of the hard truths we'd prefer to ignore, and everything else in the world that might broaden our horizons. Stuck in our own little sycophantic universes, we'll be isolated, only dimly aware that other people exist or that we might need to work together with them in a shared world.

Or maybe not. The hyperlink has the magical ability to expose us to something completely different in just a single click. Different people have different information needs, and without algorithmic filtering systems we'd be lost in the flood of the web. And anyway, was traditional, non-personalized news really that good at diversity?

People have been *talking* about the dangers of personalized algorithmic filters since the dawn of the web and we're still talking about it. We can order another round and argue about this forever, or we can try some new things.

1. Stop Speculating and Start Looking

When we look at how people interact on the web, what do we actually see? It's now possible to visualize the data trails left by communities.

On Amazon, Orgnet showed that most people buy "conservative" or "liberal" books but not both by mapping the "people who read X also read Y" recommendations. On Facebook, a 2008 analysis showed that, yes, our "friends" are more likely to agree with our political attitudes than random strangers—17 percent more likely to be exact. But it also showed that we tend to imagine our friends to be much more like us than they really are, thus inflating our *perception* of a filter bubble. On Twitter, people who tweet political terms break into left- and right-leaning social network clusters.

But these sorts of studies cannot answer questions of cause and effect. Do filtered media worlds cause the online segregation we see, or do people construct self-reinforcing filters because they already have divergent beliefs?

This is why the recent Facebook study of link sharing is so unusual: it's a comparative experiment to determine whether seeing a link in your Facebook news feed makes you more likely to share it. Drawing from a pool of 250 million users and 73 million URLs, Facebook researchers hid certain links from the control group, experimentally removing the effect of seeing that link on Facebook. This breaks the line of causation, which makes it possible to estimate, by comparison, the true influence of the algorithmically customized news feed on your behavior.

The results, summarized by Farhad Manjoo at Slate, aren't a ringing validation of the filter bubble argument. Unsurprisingly, people are more likely to share links posted by close friends, where "close" is counted (algorithmically) in terms of number of recent likes, comments, etc. But because most people have many more distant friends than close friends, most of what the news feed actually influences us to share comes from weak ties, not strong ones. In other words, the news feed tends to prompt us to view and re-share information from the edges of our social network, not the center.

This study has its limitations: it tracks all URLs shared, not just "news." Maybe we're happy to share cat pictures from random folks, but we only trust close friends when it comes to political issues. Still, I'm holding it up as an example because it's both empirical (it looks at the real world) and experimental (by comparing to a control group we can determine causation.) It might be the largest media effects study ever undertaken, and if we're serious about understanding the filter bubble we need more work like this.

Simultaneously, I think we also need to be studying older forms of media. It's not enough to compare what we have now with some idealization of the past; let's really look critically at the broadcast media era to better understand the tradeoffs now being made. There's a strong argument that mainstream news only ever really represented the concerns of white, middle-class men, and of course it used to be much harder to consciously seek out alternative perspectives. But nobody ever talks about the "filter bubble of the 1960s."

2. Bring Curation into Journalism

Editors still command attention. Every time someone subscribes in any medium, whether that's in print or on Twitter, they are giving an editor license to direct their attention in some small way. Every time an article page includes a list of suggested stories, someone is directing attention. Editors can use this donated attention to puncture filter bubbles in ways people will appreciate.

But if there has been a decline in the power of editors to set the agenda for public discussion, maybe that's because the world has gotten a lot bigger. A news editor has always been a sort of filter, making choices to cover particular stories and selecting their placement and prominence. But they filter only the product of their own newsroom, while many others are filtering the entire web. How can users depend on a filter who ignores most of everything?

Editors could become curators, cultivating the best work from both inside and outside the newsroom. A good curator rewards us for delegating our attentional choices to them. We still like to give this job to people instead of machines, because people are smart, creative, idiosyncratic, and above all personal. We can form a relationship with a good curator, sometimes even a two-way relationship when we can use social networks to start a conversation with them at any moment.

But traditional journalism isn't really in this game. For a start, curation simply wasn't possible in broadcast and print, because those media don't have hyperlinks. News organizations tied to those media have been very slow to understand and embrace links and linking. Meanwhile, the classic "link roundup" continues to thrive as online form, social media has created a new class of curation stars such as Maria Popova and Andy Carvin, and there are hugely popular news sources that mostly curate (Buzzfeed) or *only* curate (BreakingNews).

There are many possible reasons why linking and curation have not been more fully adopted by traditional news organizations, but at heart I suspect it boils down to cultural issues and anxieties about authorship . There are glorious exceptions, such as Reuters' Counterparties, which captures what Felix Salmon and Ryan McCarthy are reading. I'd love to know what other good reporters find noteworthy; that information would be at least as valuable to me as the articles they eventually produce. I believe there's still a vital role for human "filters," but only if they're willing to direct my attention to other people's work.

3. Build Better Filtering Algorithms

Filtering algorithms are here to stay, and we can make them better. In his book, Pariser suggests a diversity control on our news reading applications:

Alternatively, Google or Facebook could place a slider bar running from "only stuff I like" to "stuff other people like that I'll probably hate" at the top of search results and the News Feed, allowing users to set their own balance between tight personalization and a more diverse information flow.

I really like the concept of giving users simple controls over their personalized filters, but it's a monumental UI and technical challenge. We can throw around phrases like "my newsreader should show me more diverse viewpoints," but it's really hard to translate that into code, because we're not being very specific.

The task comes down to finding an algorithmic definition of diversity, and there are several avenues we could explore. Most recommendation systems try to maximize the chance that you'll like what you get (that is, literally "like" it, or click on it, or rate it five stars, or whatever.) This is an essentially conservative approach. Instead, a filtering algorithm could continually explore the boundaries of your interests, looking for what you didn't know you wanted. Luckily, this idea has mathematical form: We can borrow ideas from statistics and information theory and say that the algorithm should sample the space of possible items in a way that reduces uncertainty fastest.

Reddit already uses this idea in its comments filtering system, which asks users to vote items up or down. But you can't vote on comments you never see, which tends to trap voting-based filtering systems in a popularity feedback loop. In 2009, Reddit found a better answer: take into account the number of people who have actually laid eyes on the comment, and "treat the vote count as a statistical sampling of a hypothetical full vote by everyone, much as in an opinion poll," as Randall Munroe of xkcd fame explains (with pictures!) What's really going on here is that the filtering algorithm takes into account what it doesn't yet know about its audience, and tries to find out quickly; the math is here.

Another possibility is to analyze social networks to look for alternate perspectives on whatever you're reading. If people in our personal social network all hold similar opinions, our filters could trawl for what people are reading *outside* of our home cluster, retrieving items which match our interests but aren't on our social horizon. I suspect such an algorithm could be built from a mashup of document similarity and cluster analysis techniques.

There's huge scope for possible filtering algorithms. But there isn't much scope for non-engineers to experiment with them, or engineers who don't work at Google and Facebook. What I'd really like to see is an ecology of custom filters, a thriving marketplace for different ways of selecting what we see. Then we could curate filtering algorithms just as we curate sources! This idea seems to have been most fully articulated by digital humanities scholar Dan Cohen in his PressForward platform.

4. Don't Just Filter, Map

I think a lot about how to design better filters, and I always run into the same basic problem: I'm just not sure how to decide how someone's horizons should be broadened. There is far more that is important, a far greater number of issues that really matter, than one person could possibly keep up with. So how are we to make the choice of what someone *should* see on any given day? I have no good answer to this. But I see another approach: Don't try to choose for someone else. Instead, just make the possibilities clear to them.

We have no maps of the web. We have no visceral sense of its scale and richness. The great failing of search algorithms is that they only give you what you ask for, but I want a picture of the entire discoverable universe. This is the core idea behind the Overview Project, where my team and I are building a visualization system to help investigative journalists sort though huge quantities of unstructured text documents.

So what if news readers included a map of available items, and the relationships between them?

Now imagine a "You Are Here" marker on the map, highlighting books (or articles) that you've already read. Pariser argues that curiosity is the sense that you're missing something — but we're *always* missing something, and we're always part of a community that is isolated from others. Let's make those truths palpable in our information consumption systems. There are many concrete ways to do this.

In physical space, we can stare at a map of the world and find ourselves on it. We can tap our finger on where we came from, and realize how much we have yet to see. It is this experience that I want to replicate online.

5. Figure Out What We Really Want

The filter bubble is a pretty abstract concept. It needs concrete examples for illustration, but pretty much all of the examples offered so far have come down a concern that the American left and right will become increasingly isolated from one another, unable to work together to solve common problems.

This *is* a concern, because American politicians and public alike really have become more divisive and polarized over the last several decades. But if the goal is less polarization, the filter bubble is several steps removed. Addressing polarization by addressing the filter bubble is a plan that depends on a lot of big assumptions: You have to believe that the filter bubble causes or enables social segregation by politics, that exposing people to content from alternate political viewpoints will reduce political extremism, and that there isn't some other, more direct or effective way we could deal with polarization. For example, our personal relationships change us far more than any "information" we consume, so maybe we should be talking about connecting people, not content. If we want to address political polarization, then we should start asking questions at the beginning, rather than immediately assuming that filter bubbles are the issue.

Conversely, the filter bubble concept seems like it should apply to a lot more than American politics. Pariser might imagine that a good filter gives a nice balance of liberal and conservative views, but what about more unorthodox philosophies? What about things that aren't politics at all? Maybe a diverse filter should tell me about the environmental effects of bees, or the innovations of Polish cinema. For that matter, I haven't heard anyone mention language bubbles, which are far more pervasive and invisible. Why don't my filters show me more material that was translated from Chinese? In a global era, exposing different countries and cultures to each other might ultimately be a far more important goal.

These two questions have been in the background of the filter bubble discussion, but they should be central. First, what is the scope of "diversity"? Does it mean more than domestic political attitudes? Are domestic politics even the example we should be worrying about most? Second, what is it that we are trying to accomplish? How would we know if we were successful? Why do we believe that changing our filters is the best way forward? If we can't answer these questions, then we have no basis to create better filters.

> *" Inside our bubble, we are selectively exposed to information aligned with our beliefs. That is an ideal scenario to maximize engagement, but a detrimental one for developing healthy skepticism."*

Technology Can Save Us from Lies Online

Filippo Menczer

In the following viewpoint, Filippo Menczer argues that we should invest resources in the fight against the spread of misinformation. Existing in the echo chambers of filter bubbles allows us to become more gullible and thus more likely to believe misinformation. Although solutions aren't available yet, technology in the form of artificial intelligence systems could distinguish between true and false stories in the future. The author calls on computer scientists, economists, and journalists to work toward solving the problem before it is too late. Menczer is a professor of computer science and informatics at Indiana University, and also director of the Center for Complex Networks and Systems Research.

As you read, consider the following questions:

1. What is political astroturfing?
2. Did the Pope endorse Donald Trump or Hillary Clinton?
3. What is the name of the platform the author is building to study the spread of fake stories?

I f you get your news from social media, as most Americans do, you are exposed to a daily dose of hoaxes, rumors, conspiracy theories and misleading news. When it's all mixed in with reliable information from honest sources, the truth can be very hard to discern.

In fact, my research team's analysis of data from Columbia University's Emergent rumor tracker suggests that this misinformation is just as likely to go viral as reliable information.

Many are asking whether this onslaught of digital misinformation affected the outcome of the 2016 U.S. election. The truth is we do not know, although there are reasons to believe it is entirely possible, based on past analysis and accounts from other countries. Each piece of misinformation contributes to the shaping of our opinions. Overall, the harm can be very real: If people can be conned into jeopardizing our children's lives, as they do when they opt out of immunizations, why not our democracy?

As a researcher on the spread of misinformation through social media, I know that limiting news fakers' ability to sell ads, as recently announced by Google and Facebook, is a step in the right direction. But it will not curb abuses driven by political motives.

Exploiting social media

About 10 years ago, my colleagues and I ran an experiment in which we learned 72 percent of college students trusted links that appeared to originate from friends—even to the point of entering personal login information on phishing sites. This widespread vulnerability suggested another form of malicious manipulation:

INFORMATION JUNK FOOD FROM SOCIAL MEDIA

When it comes to content, Google and Facebook are offering us too much candy, and not enough carrots.

That's according to political activist and former MoveOn.org executive director Eli Pariser, who warned that the "invisible algorithmic editing of the web" via personalized search results, news feeds and other customized content is threatening to limit our exposure to new information and narrow our outlook....

...Companies have billed the personalization of information as a way of serving up content that is more relevant to a user's interests. When it rolled out personalized search to all users, Google boasted the feature would "[help] people get better search results." According to *The Facebook Effect*, Mark Zuckerberg explained the utility of Facebook's "News Feed" by telling his staff, "A squirrel dying in front of your house may be more relevant to your interests right now than people dying in Africa."

Pariser appealed to tech executives from companies like Facebook and Google present at the TED conference to reconsider their approach in order to create the internet "that we all dreamed of it being"—one introducing us to alternate, novel perspectives that challenge us to think in new ways.

"We really need you to make sure that these algorithms have encoded in them a sense of the public life, a sense of civic responsibility," Pariser said. "The thing is that the algorithms don't yet have the kind of embedded ethics that the editors did. So if algorithms are going to curate the world for us, if they're going to decide what we get to see and what we don't get to see, then we need to make sure that they're not just keyed to relevance. We need to make sure that they also show us things that are uncomfortable or challenging or important."

Smarter, more "concerned" algorithms are necessary to ensure we have a balanced information diet, Pariser said.

"The best editing gives us a bit of both," he said. "It gives us a little bit of Justin Bieber and a little bit of Afghanistan. It gives us some information vegetables and it gives us some information dessert."

continued on page 180

continued from page 179

Otherwise, he warned, we risk consuming too much "fast food" content.

"Instead of a balanced information information diet, you can end up surrounded by information junk food," Pariser said.

"Facebook, Google Giving Us Information Junk Food, Eli Pariser Warns," by Bianca Bosker, Times Internet Limited, May 26, 2011.

People might also believe misinformation they receive when clicking on a link from a social contact.

To explore that idea, I created a fake web page with random, computer-generated gossip news—things like "Celebrity X caught in bed with Celebrity Y!" Visitors to the site who searched for a name would trigger the script to automatically fabricate a story about the person. I included on the site a disclaimer, saying the site contained meaningless text and made-up "facts." I also placed ads on the page. At the end of the month, I got a check in the mail with earnings from the ads. That was my proof: Fake news could make money by polluting the internet with falsehoods.

Sadly, I was not the only one with this idea. Ten years later, we have an industry of fake news and digital misinformation. Clickbait sites manufacture hoaxes to make money from ads, while so-called hyperpartisan sites publish and spread rumors and conspiracy theories to influence public opinion.

This industry is bolstered by how easy it is to create social bots, fake accounts controlled by software that look like real people and therefore can have real influence. Research in my lab uncovered many examples of fake grassroots campaigns, also called political astroturfing.

In response, we developed the BotOrNot tool to detect social bots. It's not perfect, but accurate enough to uncover persuasion campaigns in the Brexit and antivax movements. Using BotOrNot, our colleagues found that a large portion of online chatter about the 2016 elections was generated by bots.

Creating Information Bubbles

We humans are vulnerable to manipulation by digital misinformation thanks to a complex set of social, cognitive, economic and algorithmic biases. Some of these have evolved for good reasons: Trusting signals from our social circles and rejecting information that contradicts our experience served us well when our species adapted to evade predators. But in today's shrinking online networks, a social network connection with a conspiracy theorist on the other side of the planet does not help inform my opinions.

Copying our friends and unfollowing those with different opinions give us echo chambers so polarized that researchers can tell with high accuracy whether you are liberal or conservative by just looking at your friends. The network structure is so dense that any misinformation spreads almost instantaneously within one group, and so segregated that it does not reach the other.

Inside our bubble, we are selectively exposed to information aligned with our beliefs. That is an ideal scenario to maximize engagement, but a detrimental one for developing healthy skepticism. Confirmation bias leads us to share a headline without even reading the article.

Our lab got a personal lesson in this when our own research project became the subject of a vicious misinformation campaign in the run-up to the 2014 U.S. midterm elections. When we investigated what was happening, we found fake news stories about our research being predominantly shared by Twitter users within one partisan echo chamber, a large and homogeneous community of politically active users. These people were quick to retweet and impervious to debunking information.

Viral Inevitability

Our research shows that given the structure of our social networks and our limited attention, it is inevitable that some memes will go viral, irrespective of their quality. Even if individuals tend to share information of higher quality, the network as a whole is not effective at discriminating between reliable and fabricated information. This helps explain all the viral hoaxes we observe in the wild.

The attention economy takes care of the rest: If we pay attention to a certain topic, more information on that topic will be produced. It's cheaper to fabricate information and pass it off as fact than it is to report actual truth. And fabrication can be tailored to each group: Conservatives read that the pope endorsed Trump, liberals read that he endorsed Clinton. He did neither.

Beholden to Algorithms

Since we cannot pay attention to all the posts in our feeds, algorithms determine what we see and what we don't. The algorithms used by social media platforms today are designed to prioritize engaging posts—ones we're likely to click on, react to and share. But a recent analysis found intentionally misleading pages got at least as much online sharing and reaction as real news.

This algorithmic bias toward engagement over truth reinforces our social and cognitive biases. As a result, when we follow links shared on social media, we tend to visit a smaller, more homogeneous set of sources than when we conduct a search and visit the top results.

Existing research shows that being in an echo chamber can make people more gullible about accepting unverified rumors. But we need to know a lot more about how different people respond to a single hoax: Some share it right away, others fact-check it first.

We are simulating a social network to study this competition between sharing and fact-checking. We are hoping to help untangle conflicting evidence about when fact-checking helps stop hoaxes from spreading and when it doesn't. Our preliminary results suggest that the more segregated the community of hoax believers, the longer the hoax survives. Again, it's not just about the hoax itself but also about the network.

Many people are trying to figure out what to do about all this. According to Mark Zuckerberg's latest announcement, Facebook teams are testing potential options. And a group of college students has proposed a way to simply label shared links as "verified" or not.

Some solutions remain out of reach, at least for the moment. For example, we can't yet teach artificial intelligence systems how to discern between truth and falsehood. But we can tell ranking algorithms to give higher priority to more reliable sources.

Studying the Spread of Fake News

We can make our fight against fake news more efficient if we better understand how bad information spreads. If, for example, bots are responsible for many of the falsehoods, we can focus attention on detecting them. If, alternatively, the problem is with echo chambers, perhaps we could design recommendation systems that don't exclude differing views.

To that end, our lab is building a platform called Hoaxy to track and visualize the spread of unverified claims and corresponding fact-checking on social media. That will give us real-world data, with which we can inform our simulated social networks. Then we can test possible approaches to fighting fake news.

Hoaxy may also be able to show people how easy it is for their opinions to be manipulated by online information—and even how likely some of us are to share falsehoods online. Hoaxy will join a suite of tools in our Observatory on Social Media, which allows anyone to see how memes spread on Twitter. Linking tools like these to human fact-checkers and social media platforms could make it easier to minimize duplication of efforts and support each other.

It is imperative that we invest resources in the study of this phenomenon. We need all hands on deck: Computer scientists, social scientists, economists, journalists and industry partners must work together to stand firm against the spread of misinformation.

> *"If we believe that news has a civic role—that it is something at least somewhat distinct from entertainment and has purposes other than making money—then we need more principled answers to the question of who should see what when."*

Online Content Should Be Personalized in an Entirely Different Way

Jonathan Stray

In the following viewpoint, Jonathan Stray argues that there is simply too much news available for any of us to consume. The author puts forward the idea that mass media can improve its management of making news available to readers. How can the news be edited and curated to serve people better? The first step is to understand that it boils down to attention: What kind of news will people spend time consuming? Unfortunately, that is a difficult question to answer. The author suggests that to decide who sees what, and when, we need to determine who is interested in a story, the span of the story's effect, and the ability of the story to facilitate change. Stray teaches computational journalism at Columbia University and leads the Overview Project for the Associated Press.

As you read, consider the following questions:

1. How many original stories does the Associated Press produce every day?
2. What definition of a "public" does the author highlight?
3. Why does the author think journalism should free itself from focusing on "what just happened"?

I really don't know how a news editor should choose what stories to put in front of people, because I don't think it's possible to cram the entire world into headlines. The publisher of a major international newspaper once told me that he delivers "the five or six things I absolutely have to know this morning." But there was always a fundamental problem with that idea, which the Internet has made starkly obvious: There is far more that matters than any one of us can follow. In most cases, the limiting factor in journalism is not what was reported but the attention we can pay to it.

Yet we still need news. Something's got to give. So what if we abandon the idea that everyone sees the same stories? That was a pre-Internet technological limitation, and maybe we've let what was possible become what is right. I want to recognize that each person not only has unique interests, but is uniquely affected by larger events, and has a unique capacity to act.

If not every person sees the same news at the same time, then the question becomes: Who should see what when? It's a hard question. It's a question of editorial choice, of filter design, of what kind of civic discussion we will have. It's the basic question we face as we embrace the network's ability to deliver individually tailored information. I propose three simple answers. You should see a story if:

- You specifically go looking for it.
- It affects you or any of your communities.
- There is something you might be able to do about it.

Interest, effects, agency. These are three ways that a story might intersect with you, and they are reasons you might need to see it.

But turn them around and they say: if a story doesn't interest me, doesn't affect me, and there's nothing I could do anyway, then I don't need to see it. What about broadening our horizons? What about a shared view of unfolding history? The idea that we will each have an individualized view on the world can be somewhat unsettling, but insisting on a single news agenda has its own disadvantages. Before getting into detailed design principles for personalized news, I want to look at how bad the information overload problem actually is, and how we came to believe in mass media.

Too Much That Matters

A solid daily newspaper might run a couple hundred items per day, just barely readable from cover to cover. Meanwhile, The Associated Press produces about 15,000 original text stories every day (and syndicates many times that number)—far more than one person can consume. But the giants of journalism are dwarfed by the collaborative authorship of the Internet. There are currently 72 hours of video uploaded to YouTube every minute, which now houses more video than was produced during the entire 20th century. There are 400 million tweets per day, meaning that if only one tweet in a million was worthwhile you could still spend your entire day on Twitter. There are several times more web pages than people in the world.

All of this available information is a tiny fraction of everything that *could* be reported. It's impossible to estimate what fraction of stories go "unreported," because there is no way to count stories before they're written; stories do not exist in nature. Yet from the point of view of the consumer, there is still far, far too much available. Ethan Zuckerman has argued that the limiting factor in foreign reporting is not journalistic resources, but the attention of the consumer. I suspect this applies to most other kinds of journalism as well; raise your hand if you've been carefully following what your city council is up to.

Compared to the news, there is simply very little attention available.

For the single-issue activist, the goal is attention at any cost. But editors have a different mission: They must choose from *all* issues. There is a huge number of potentially important stories, but only a tiny fraction can be "headlines." Most stories *must* languish in obscurity, because you or I cannot hope to read a thousandth of the journalism produced each day. But even the flood of global journalism is a tragically narrow view on the world, compared to everything on the Internet.

How, then, should an editor choose what tiny part of the world to show us? Sometimes there is an event so massive, so universal, it demands attention. Natural disasters and revolutions come to mind. For all other stories, I don't think there is an answer. We can't even agree on what problems are important. No single set of headlines can faithfully represent all that matters in the world.

There Is More Than One Public

The Internet is not like broadcast technology—print, radio, TV. But the routines and assumptions of journalism were formed under the technical constraints of the mass media era. I wonder if we have mistaken what was possible for what is desirable.

The first technical limitation I want to consider was this: Everyone had to see the same thing. This surely reinforced the seductive idea that there is only one "public." It's an especially seductive idea for those who have the ability to choose the message. But there's something here for the rest of us too. There's the idea that if you pay attention to the broadcast or read the daily paper, you're informed. You know all there is to know—or at least everything that's important, and everything everyone else knows. Whatever else it may be, this is a comforting idea.

Media theorists also love the idea of a unified public. Marshall McLuhan was enamored with the idea of the global village where the tribal drums of mass media informed all of us at the same time. Jürgen Habermas articulated the idea of the public sphere as the place where people could collectively discuss what mattered to them, but he doesn't like the Internet, calling it "millions of fragmented chat rooms."

But the idea of a unified public never really made sense. Who is "us"? A town? A political party? The "business community"? The whole world? It depends on the publication and the story, and a few 20th-century figures recognized this. In *The Public and Its Problems*, written in 1927, John Dewey provided an amazing definition of "a public": a group of people united by an issue that affects them. In fact, for Dewey a public doesn't really exist until something affects the group interest, such as a proposed law that might seriously affect the residents of a town.

We can update this definition a little bit and say that each person can belong to many different publics simultaneously. You can simultaneously be a student, Moroccan, gay, a mother, conservative, and an astronomer. These many identities won't necessarily align with political boundaries, but each can be activated if threatened by external events. Such affiliations are fluid and overlapping, and in many cases, we can actually visualize the communities built around them.

The News Isn't Just What's New

There was another serious technical limitation of 20th-century media: There was no way to go back to what was reported before. You could look at yesterday's paper if you hadn't thrown it out, or even go to the library and look up last year on microfilm. Similarly, there were radio and television archives. But it was so hard to rewind that most people never did.

Each story was meant to be viewed only once, on the day of its publication or broadcast. The news media were not, and could not be, reference media. The emphasis was therefore on what was new, and journalists still speak of "advancing the story" and the "top" versus "context" or "background" material. This makes sense for a story you can never go back to, about a topic that you can't look up. But somehow this limitation of the medium became enshrined, and journalism came to believe that only new events deserved attention, and that consuming small, daily, incremental updates is the best way to stay informed about the world.

It's not. Piecemeal updates don't work for complex stories. Wikipedia rapidly filled the explanatory gap, and the journalism profession is now rediscovering the explainer and figuring out how to give people the context they need to understand the news.

I want to go one step further and ask what happens if journalism frees itself from (only) giving people stories about "what just happened." Whole worlds open up: We can talk about long-term issues, or keep something on the front page as long as it is still relevant, or decide *not* to deliver that hot story until the user is at a point where they might want to know. Journalism could be a reference guide to the present, not just a stream of real-time events.

Design Principles for Personalized News

If we let go of the idea of single set of headlines for everyone based around current events, we get personalized news feeds which can address timescales longer than the breaking news cycle. Not everyone can afford to hire a personal editor, so we'll need a combination of human curators, social media, and sophisticated filtering algorithms to make personalized feeds possible for everyone.

Yet the people working on news personalization systems have mostly been technologists who have viewed story selection as a sort of clickthrough-optimization problem. If we believe that news has a civic role—that it is something at least somewhat distinct from entertainment and has purposes other than making money—then we need more principled answers to the question of who should see what when. Here again are my three:

Interest

Anyone who wants to know should be able to know. From a product point of view, this translates into good search and subscription features. Search is particularly important because it makes it easy to satisfy your curiosity, closing the gap between wondering and knowing. But search has proven difficult for news organizations because it inverts the editorial process of story selection and timing, putting control entirely in the hands of users—who may not be looking for the latest breaking tidbit. Journalism is still about the present, but we can't assume that every reader has been following every story, or that the "present" means "what just happened" as opposed to "what has been happening for the last decade." But for users who do decide they want to keep up to date on a particular topic, the ability to "follow" a single story would be very helpful.

Effects

I should know about things that will affect me. Local news organizations always did this, by covering what was of interest to their particular geographic community. But each of us is a member of many different communities now, mostly defined by identity or interest and not geography. Each way of seeing communities gives us a different way of understanding who might be affected by something happening in the world. Making sure that the affected people know is also a prerequisite for creating "publics," in Dewey's sense of a group of people who act together in their common interest. Journalism could use the targeting techniques pioneered by marketers to find these publics, and determine who might care about each story.

Agency

Ultimately, I believe journalism must facilitate change. Otherwise, what's the point? This translates to the idea of agency, the idea that someone can be empowered by knowing. But not every person can affect every thing, because people differ in position, capability, and authority. So my third principle is this: Anyone who might be able to act on a story should see it. This applies regardless of whether or not that person is directly affected, which makes it the most social and empathetic of these principles. For example, a politician needs to know about the effects of a factory being built in a city they do not live in, and if disaster recovery efforts can benefit from random donations then everyone has agency and everyone should know. Further, the right time for me to see a story is not necessarily when the story happens, but when I might be able to act.

These are not the only reasons anyone should ever see a story. Beyond these principles, there is a whole world of cultural awareness and expanded horizons, the vast other. There are ways to bring more diversity into our filters, but the criteria are much less clear because this is fundamentally an aesthetic choice; there is no right path through culture. At least we can say that a personalized news feed designed according to the above principles will keep each of us informed about the parts of the world that might affect us, or where we might have a chance to affect others.

Periodical and Internet Sources Bibliography

Sally Adee, "How Can Facebook and Its Users Burst the 'Filter Bubble'?" *Daily News*, November 18, 2016. https://www.newscientist.com/article/2113246-how-can-facebook-and-its-users-burst-the-filter-bubble/.

Lettie Y. Conrad, "Embrace the Bubble... or Burst It?" Scholarly Kitchen, December 22, 2016. https://scholarlykitchen.sspnet.org/2016/12/22/bubble-or-burst/.

Cory Doctorow, "Theresa May Promises a British Version of Iran's Halal Internet," Boing Boing, May 19, 2017. http://boingboing.net/2017/05/19/little-england-little-internet.html.

Stuart Dredge, "Digital Politics: Are We Trapped Within Our Online Filter Bubbles?" *Guardian*, November 11, 2015. https://www.theguardian.com/technology/2015/nov/11/digital-politics-online-filter-bubbles.

Alison Flood, "JK Rowling Presses the Case Against Scottish Independence," *Guardian*, September 8, 2014. https://www.theguardian.com/books/2014/sep/08/jk-rowling-against-scottish-independence-harry-potter.

Mike Godwin and Tom Struble, "Don't Freak Out About the FCC's New Approach to Net Neutrality," Slate, May 23, 2017. http://www.slate.com/articles/technology/future_tense/2017/05/don_t_freak_out_about_the_fcc_s_new_approach_to_net_neutrality.html.

Alex Hern, "Facebook Doesn't Need to Ban Fake News to Fight It," *Guardian*, November 25, 2016. https://www.theguardian.com/technology/2016/nov/25/facebook-fake-news-fight-mark-zuckerberg.

John Lanchester, "You Are the Product," *London Review of Books*, Vol. 39 No. 16, August 17, 2017. https://www.lrb.co.uk/v39/n16/john-lanchester/you-are-the-product.

David Lumb, "Why Scientists Are Upset About the Facebook Filter Bubble Story," Fast Company, August 5, 2015. https://www.fastcompany.com/3046111/why-scientists-are-upset-over-the-facebook-filter-bubble-study.

Diana Mehta, "Ottawa Student Denounces 'Rape Culture' in Wake of Facebook Hate," *Chronicle Herald*, March 2, 2014. http://

thechronicleherald.ca/canada/1190780-ottawa-student-denounces-rape-culture-in-wake-of-facebook-hate.

@NobelPrize. "The Research Counts, Not the Journal." Twitter, June 22, 2017. https://twitter.com/NobelPrize/status/877804020345262080.

Brendan Nyhan, "The Challenge of False Beliefs: Understanding and Countering Misperceptions in Politics and Health Care," Conference on How We Can Improve Health Science Communication, June 13, 2016. https://www.isr.umich.edu/cps/events/Nyhan_20160613.PDF.

For Further Discussion

Chapter 1

1. Are online filters operating according to good business practices? Why or why not?
2. Who is in charge of personal internet use? Is that always true? Give examples to make your case.
3. What are internet filters doing differently from the choices a person makes online?

Chapter 2

1. Are internet filters helpful to a casual internet and online media user? Give examples.
2. How are filters affecting the ways people use search engines?
3. What is being done with all the personal data gathered online?

Chapter 3

1. Is your social media use improved in any way by internet filters?
2. Have you changed your use of online media because of what you've heard about filters? Why or why not?
3. Do formal scientific studies of online filters mean more to you than informal articles by a reporter?

Chapter 4

1. How can a person use the Internet without being influenced much by filters? Provide concrete examples.
2. What government legislation affecting internet filters is appropriate to support, and why?
3. What computers, programs, browsers, and websites are good choices for people trying to protect their personal information?

Organizations to Contact

The editors have compiled the following list of organizations concerned with the issues debated in this book. The descriptions are derived from materials provided by the organizations. All have publications or information available for interested readers. The list was compiled on the date of publication of the present volume; the information provided here may change. Be aware that many organizations take several weeks or longer to respond to inquiries, so allow as much time as possible.

Artstor

2 Rector Street, 18th floor
New York, NY 10006
(899) 771-4908
email: artstor.org/form/contact-us
website: www.artstor.org

Artstor is a nonprofit with a mission to use digital images and media to enhance scholarship and education. The association brings together more than two million high-quality images for education and research and offers the tools to catalog, manage, and distribute digital media collections. The association maintains a newsletter as well as a blog with news on photojournalism and links to online data and image collections.

Aspen Ideas Festival

Aspen Institute
PO Box 222
Queenstown, MD 21658
(805) 962-9412
email: info@aspeninstitute.org
website: www.aspenideas.org

The Aspen Ideas Festival is a major American conference and public gathering place for leaders from around the globe and across many disciplines. At the festival, they engage in deep and inquisitive discussion of the ideas and issues that both shape our lives and challenge our times. Some 350 presenters, 200 sessions, and 3,000 attendees comprise the annual festival, launched in 2005, on the Aspen Institute's campus in Aspen, Colorado.

Congress of the Humanities and Social Sciences

Federation for the Humanities and Social Sciences/Fédération des sciences humaines
Suite 300, 275 Bank Street
Ottawa, ON K2P 2L6
Canada
(613) 238-6112
email: federation@ideas-idees.ca
website: www.ideas-idees.ca

The Federation for the Humanities and Social Sciences promotes research and teaching for the advancement of an inclusive, democratic, and prosperous society. With a membership now comprising over 160 universities, colleges, and scholarly associations, the federation represents a diverse community of ninety-one thousand researchers and graduate students across Canada in both official languages (English and French).

Future Tense

Slate New York office
15 MetroTech Center, 8th Floor
Brooklyn, NY 11201
(212) 445-5330
email: slateoffice@slate.com
website: www.slate.com/blogs/future_tense.html

A partnership of Slate, New America, and Arizona State University, Future Tense explores how emerging technologies will change the way we live, focusing on the longer-term transformative power of robotics, information and communication technologies, synthetic biology, augmented reality, and space exploration. Future Tense also examines whether technology and its development can be governed democratically and ethically.

JSTOR Daily

JSTOR
ITHAKA office
2 Rector Street, 18th floor
New York, NY 10006
(888)388-3574
email: www.jstor.org/forms/content/jstor-help-support
website: www/jstor.org

JSTOR is a digital library for scholars, researchers, and students providing access to more than ten million journal articles, books, and primary sources in seventy-five disciplines. JSTOR collaborates with the academic community to help libraries connect patrons to vital content while lowering costs and increasing shelf space, provides independent researchers with free and low-cost access to scholarship, and helps publishers reach new audiences and preserve their content for future generations.

Medium

760 Market Street, Suite 900
San Francisco, CA 94102
email: yourfriends@medium.com
website: www.medium.com

Medium is an open platform without advertising for writers around the world to use for posting their own written stories. Readers can subscribe to be notified when a particular writer posts a new story. Readers can also follow tags to get stories about their favorite topics. Staff editors select some stories that are made publicly available and showcase them at https://medium.com/topic/editors-picks.

National Public Radio

1111 North Capitol Street NE
Washington, DC
(202) 513-2031
website: www.npr.org

National Public Radio is a multimedia news network and radio program producer, with stations and supporters across the United States. NPR presents independent journalism that examines diverse perspectives. Much of the programming is available online and archived. With staff in dozens of bureaus nationally and internationally, NPR has become an essential news source tracking complex issues over the long term.

Reputation.com

1400A Seaport Boulevard, Suite 401
Redwood City, CA 94063
email: reputation.com/contact
website: www.reputation.com

Reputation.com helps large organizations with hundreds or thousands of consumer-facing locations ensure that their star ratings and reviews reflect the truth about the services they provide. Based in California's Silicon Valley with offices in Arizona, Europe, and Asia, the team is funded by the same venture capital firms that backed Skype, Intuit, and Symantec. Their patented technology gives clients the power to drive up ratings and reviews, make operational improvements, and accelerate recurring visits and revenue.

Social Media Camp

website: https://socialmediacamp.ca

Social Media Camp is Canada's largest social media conference, attracting a broad spectrum of delegates. Attendees come from all over North America and from all sectors of the economy—small business, large business, government, education, and nonprofit —to tackle all aspects of social media.

TED talks

TED Conferences LLC
330 Hudson Street, 11th Floor
New York, NY 10013
(212) 346-9333
email: support.ted.com/customer/portal/emails/new
website: www.ted.com/talks

TED is a nonprofit devoted to spreading ideas, usually in the form of short, powerful talks (eighteen minutes or less). TED began in 1984 as a conference where technology, entertainment and design converged and today covers almost all topics—from science to business to global issues—in more than one hundred languages. Meanwhile, independently run TEDx events help share ideas in communities around the world.

Worldcon

World Science Fiction Convention
World Science Fiction Society
PO Box 64128
Sunnyvale CA 94088
email: worldcon.org/contact
website: www.worldcon.org

Worldcon is the annual convention of the World Science Fiction Society (WSFS). The subject matter presented in programming includes not only science fiction books and media but speculative ideas and how they affect people. This series of international conferences is far more accessible to lay people than academic conferences and can encourage learners to discuss ideas and current events with an open mind.

Bibliography of Books

Sven Birkerts. *Changing the Subject: Art and Attention in the Internet Age*. Minneapolis, MN: Greywolf Press, 2015.

Danah Boyd. *It's Complicated: The Social Lives of Networked Teens*. New Haven, CT: Yale University Press, 2015.

Nicholas Carr. *The Glass Cage: How Our Computers Are Changing Us*. New York, NY: WW Norton, 2015.

James Curran, Natalie Fenton, and Des Freedman. *Misunderstanding the Internet*. New York, NY: Routledge, 2016.

Cory Doctorow. *Information Doesn't Want to Be Free: Laws for the Internet Age*. San Francisco, CA: McSweeney's Publishing, 2015.

Howard Gardner and Katie Davis. *The App Generation: How Today's Youth Navigate Identity, Intimacy, and Imagination in a Digital World*. New Haven, CT: Yale University Press, 2014.

Susan Greenfield. *Mind Change: How Digital Technologies Are Leaving Their Mark on Our Brains*. New York, NY: Random House, 2015.

Lisa Guernsey and Michael H. Levine. *Tap, Click, Read: Growing Readers in a World of Screenz*. Hoboken, NJ: Wiley, 2015.

Trevor MacKenzie. *Dive into Inquiry: Amplify Learning and Empower Student Voice*. Ivine, CA: EdTechTeam Press, 2016.

John Palfrey. *BiblioTech: Why Libraries Matter More Than Ever in the Age of Google*. New York, NY: Basic Books, 2015.

Eli Pariser. *The Filter Bubble: How the New Personalized Web Is Changing What We Read and How We Think*. New York, NY: Penguin Press, 2012.

Thomas E. Patterson. *Informing the News: The Need For Knowledge-Based Journalism*. New York, NY: Vintage, 2013.

Lars Roper. *Locher: Life and Death in My Personalized Internet Hole*. Amazon Digital Services, 2012

Timothy Snyder. *On Tyranny: Twenty Lessons from the Twentieth Century*. New York, NY: Penguin/Random House, 2017.

Seth Stevens-Davidowitz. *Everybody Lies: Big Data, New Data, and What the Internet Can Tell Us About Who We Really Are*. New York NY: Dey Street Books/ Harpercollins, 2017.

Jonathan Taplin. *Move Fast and Break Things*. London, UK: Macmillan, 2017.

Katherine Tarbox. *A Girl's Life Online*. New York, NY: Penguin/ Random House, 2017.

Daniel Trottier. *Social Media as Surveillance: Rethinking Visibility in a Converging World*. Farnham, UK: Ashgate, 2012.

Tom Vanderbilt. *You May Also Like: Taste in an Age of Endless Choice*. New York, NY: Knopf 2016

Mary Wollstonecraft Shelley, David H. Guston, Ed Finn, and Jason Scott Robert, editors. *Frankenstein: Annotated for Scientists, Engineers, and Creators of All Kinds*. Cambridge, MA: MIT Press, 2017.

Tim Wu. *The Attention Merchants: The Epic Scramble to Get Inside Our Heads*. New York, NY: Knopf, 2016.

Tim Wu. *The Master Switch: Rise and Fall of Information Empires*. New York, NY: Vintage, 2011.

Index